When Writing Morphs into a Lifetime

A NOVEL

MYRNA LOU JASTRA

authorHOUSE®

AuthorHouse™
1663 Liberty Drive
Bloomington, IN 47403
www.authorhouse.com
Phone: 1 (800) 839-8640

Published by AuthorHouse   09/19/2017

ISBN: 978-1-5246-9780-8 (sc)
ISBN: 978-1-5246-9781-5 (hc)
ISBN: 978-1-5246-9779-2 (e)

Library of Congress Control Number: 2017910116

Print information available on the last page.

G RACE, THE UNIVERSITY PUBLICATION'S OFFICE administrative assistant, called the attention of a young sophomore who seemed to be in a rush, "Lor, you have mail. Aren't you from that city? Isn't that your home?" Grace pointed at the envelope's return address.

"Thanks," Lor said and nodded.

Only when Lor arrived at her dormitory did she find time to open the mail, an invitation dated August 30, 1948, from an editor of an all-boys military academy, asking her to write for their school's special issue.

Lor found it puzzling. She never had an acquaintance with anyone among that school's editors. She read through the letter again:

> In line with our policy of dedicating a number yearly for the fair sex, we have decided to make our November issue entirely feminine. For this purpose, our official publication's staff is requesting your assistance in putting this issue out successfully. Please send us your short story, poems, essays (preferably humorous ones), and whatever contributions you think of. We have set the deadline for October 1,

inasmuch as the printing of our magazine is done in Manila. Kindly accompany your articles with your picture. Your cooperation will be highly appreciated.

Ermin Oro, the femmes editor, signed the letter on behalf of *The Corps*, the official publication of the Philippine Military Academy in the city of Baguio, Lor's hometown.

After a week, a phone call came. Gloria approached Lor in the midst of acknowledging receipt of her just-delivered laundry and asked her to hold the line. The caller identified himself as the incoming editor of a publication. Lor recalled the name.

"I have only ten minutes to explain my request. Did you receive the letter mailed to the office of your university's publication?" the caller queried.

Lor was visibly miffed by the call. She was feeling a sense of guilt. "Yes. I'm sorry I was not able to reply to you immediately. I had my midterm exams and three term papers to write. But I'll respond in writing tomorrow."

The caller, who further identified himself, seemed relieved. But as he continued the conversation, he informed Lor how photos were requested to accompany all contributions. He seemed friendlier as they continued their phone conversation. Lor assured him she would answer queries in less than ten minutes.

Lor told Ermin Oro how she doubted very much if a picture of hers would do justice to photography and assured him two pieces bearing her authorship would be in the mail the next day. Living up to her word, Lor sent a short story and an essay accompanied by a school picture on September 14, 1948:

> I am sending a picture. It is a copy of my ID as a representative of our school paper. As I have told you, I doubt very much if it does justice to photography. I have enclosed a short story. It is not humorous. And if you believe that it cannot be published in the November issue, I shall understand. Please send it back to me. Kindly pick out what you believe will suit your purpose.

The semester flew by. It was time for Lor to return to her mountain home. Attending the university in her native land's capital was far from the environment she recalled at five thousand feet above sea level. Each time she would visit Baguio, Lor had more than a tinge of sadness as she viewed the physical state of her hometown, which bore the scars of World War II.

Before December 8, 1941, her city stood alone as one of Mother Nature's favorites, unparalleled in its beauty and clean air. World War II had just come to an end in mid-1945. The city she loved was still in rubble and ruin three years later. But she was grateful that the scenery remained. Pine trees and floral beauties continued to bloom amid the cool weather that was uniquely Baguio.

November arrived. It was the end of the first semester. It was also precious time to visit home. While planning her semester break, Lor remembered an invitation to attend a social at home. The function, a hop, was a dance to join cosponsors and cadets of her university's reserved officers' unit, a welcoming gesture from another government-funded educational institution.

Lor was not at all surprised that her school's host would be the country's national military academy. Along with her college friends who were invited to join the event, Lor went to the dinner reception and dance. Dance music was heard as guests approached the venue's entrance. Their hosts escorted them to the dinner table.

The dance hall seemed bereft of familiar faces. As Lor and her company sat at their assigned tables with their place cards, cadets approached them to dance while the music went on. Band music was on target for boogie-woogie, jitterbug, guracha, rhumba, and tango. Four dance pieces in a row kept the dancers on the floor.

As soon as Lor and her tablemates were seated, one cadet approached their table and introduced himself as he eyed Lor.

"I presume you are Miss Arce," he said. "I am Cadet Oro."

Lor extended her hand.

Still standing as erect as the post behind him, Ermin continued his introductory remarks while dance music filled the hall, "I saw you dancing from afar. I don't dance that way at all. No wonder my classmates have talked about you. Your name should be Lore, with an e."

Lor felt embarrassed. She thought Ermin was aggressive as he emphasized *lore*, which was new to her. She said, "I'm not legendary." But she smiled as she felt the term *lore* was literary and reminded her of her sixth-grade English teacher, who was responsible for sending her entries to writing contests.

"Your last name means gold too. That's also part of lore," she commented.

Once more, Lor excused herself when another friend asked her to dance. It was clear that she loved dancing. Those who asked her to dance fell in line. Ermin remained behind and took one seat at their table.

Returning to the same setup, Lor joined her college group after three consecutive dance pieces. She was surprised to see Ermin still seated where she had left him. He stood from his seat. Again, he stood erect.

The evening wore on. Lor and Ermin had snatches of conversation. She found out he came from the southern tip of the country, a typhoon-ravaged region. He was the fourth of a dozen siblings. His father was an English major at the same university campus that Lor was attending, and he had taught at a language school.

Lor wanted to learn how Ermin obtained her name and address when he extended the invitation to write for the magazine that was to be off the press very soon. But she stopped herself. She would find out later. She preferred to continue dancing her favorites. Her partners proved to be excellent dancers.

Lor's timepiece indicated it was close to eleven thirty. The invitation, as she recalled, said "7:00 to 12:00 midnight." Ermin didn't ask Lor to dance at all, which was puzzling. Nor did he dance with anyone else.

As though Ermin had read her mind, he mentioned in a casual tone, "We have a dance class. Maybe it's time for me to start learning fancy steps." Then he ventured to ask, "How long will you be in town?"

"All week because it is our semester break," Lor answered.

Then the last dance piece's notes struck loudly, a waltz, *Auld Lang Syne*, as the bandleader encouraged everyone to dance. "Last call," he said.

Although it was the last dance, Ermin didn't ask for a dance. Nor did he dance at all.

Lor bade her friends good-bye and extended her hand to Ermin, who walked her to the hall's exit and off to her family car.

The next day, a Sunday, the phone rang at the Arce residence. It was Ermin. He inquired whether her vacation schedule would allow her to accommodate a brief visit that weekend. Lor informed Ermin she was having guests for an early dinner and some dancing, nothing formal, so she extended the invitation, saying he could dress casually.

Ermin came forty minutes before the scheduled time. He explained how cabs were at a high premium on Sundays and he didn't want to wait. He was dressed in the academy's uniform, nothing casual.

Lor asked for hors d'oeuvres from the kitchen while she waited for the other guests' arrival. Ermin continued to introduce himself. He made mention of his family origins— how his parents decided to move to the southern part of the country, where there were more and better business opportunities. He didn't ask about Lor's family.

Lor asked how he got his first name, Ermin. He said his mother was fond of the name, likened it to a coat, protection-wise.

Guests started to come in. One, Oscar, brought records to dance to. He also was his own accompanist as Lor asked him to play the piano while he sang love songs. The party was lively. As host, Lor had to see to everyone's comfort. Ermin seemed to flow with the crowd. He was an interesting conversationalist. But still he didn't dance at all.

The dance music came through. Lor chose all selections. She no longer considered it strange that dancing wasn't part of Ermin's life. She loved dancing. Her guests did too.

During a break in the party, Ermin asked to be excused so he could call a cab to take him back to his school's barracks. Lor offered her family car in lieu of having to obtain cab service because she was aware the wait could be long. Cabs were rare on weekends. All Baguio folks knew that.

Ermin thanked Lor for the favor, which allowed him to stay longer after a few guests remained to continue dancing. It was time to go, but others stayed behind to sing and dance. Ermin asked to be excused. His permission to be away from his barracks was slowly drawing to a close. Per Lor's suggestion, he gladly accepted her invitation that he ride back in her family car with two guests who lived near the academy.

The week went on. Three phone calls laced with brevity came from Ermin almost at the same time, close to the end of each class day.

Initially, the caller identified himself, "Plebe Bert Armada, fourth class." Continuing, he would say, "Please hold the line for Cadet Oro."

Phone conversations were what they were. Beyond the usual "How are you?" not much could be taken up because the lines for phone opportunities were not long. Calls had their fifteen-minute limits.

The day after playing host to her friends, Lor informed them how she had to fly back to the country's capital and to school.

Ermin asked, "Would it be all right to see you for a few minutes?"

Lor wondered, "Why just a few minutes?" But she didn't inquire further. Lor was beginning to understand Ermin.

He arrived after twenty minutes and asked the cab driver to wait. He ran up the Arce residence's stairway and handed an almost-weightless package to Lor with a single red rose attached to the light box. In a few minutes, he left.

Lor opened the package and found a letter that included a familiar melody and its lyrics, "Because of You." The letter spoke of Ermin's admiration for her writing, friendliness, and courtesy to her guests. There was no hint of affection. The sole mention was a one-line sentence that accompanied the melody in writing, "You are the inspiration of this song."

It made her wonder, "Was there a need to include the melody's lyrics?"

She started to compare Ermin's letter with those she had received from some admirers, including those from his own classmates whom she had met much earlier before they entered the academy. Letters and books she received from her campus friends who belonged to fraternities accompanied floral arrangements to her dormitory. Lor remembered them as large floral presents. A single flower? A song? Both from Ermin.

Since it was Lor's practice to respond to letters, she wrote a brief note, thanking Ermin for his thoughtfulness.

Four weeks passed by. No word came from him. The months wore on. A week before Christmas, she received a note from Ermin, informing Lor he was going to spend their class's first Christmas break with his family, the first-ever that all second-year cadets (yearlings) could avail of since they entered the academy. They would be granted a two-week vacation.

Before the holidays set in, Lor received the usual Christmas greeting cards from friends and acquaintances. She looked at her mail and saw a card that was larger than the others were. It was a greeting card from Ermin. Three pine tree needles and a small pine cone were attached to a short note, "Enjoy the holidays away from your school cares. I'll think of you although I'll be away from Baguio." He included his complimentary ending, "Always me," and the note bore his name. For the first time, Lor was touched.

1949 arrived on the scene. There were more letters from Ermin. He did not mention love at all. He did write on how people who cared for one another should think of commitment, the future, similarities, and differences.

Lor wrote him back. She informed him that she did aim to finish all her course requirements to allow her to apply for scholarships abroad. Her academic transcript was not straight A's but met the requirements of graduate school openings to start with a master's degree in the United States for the 1951 school year at the earliest, and 1952 at the latest.

Likewise, there was the allure of a foreign service assignment, if she were to hurdle the required examinations successfully as she was going to be awarded a bachelor of science in foreign service very soon. The thought was exciting. Lor had completed course requirements of the two bachelor degrees she worked for. In the meantime, while awaiting the outcome of her post-college applications, she wanted to work for a metropolitan daily.

She reported to the university registrar's office where the registrar, Dr. Ramon Portugal, cooperated in acquiescing to provide her official transcripts and a certificate of completion of her bachelor degrees so she could proceed with her plans for the future. Attendance at a formal commencement program was unnecessary.

Lor was exuberant. October arrived. School was over for her. She had two bachelor degrees. If she were on the quest for a job, she would need another copy of official transcripts.

She pondered, "Why not?" She knew she wanted to be in the writing field, a reporter. "A journalist perhaps?" It wouldn't hurt to approach the editor or whoever was responsible in hiring reporters, even if she had to be initially a cub reporter. Looking at the want ads did not indicate there were position vacancies for reporters.

But she had heard of the **Manila Daily Bulletin**, whose offices were on Florentino Torres Street in Manila. That paper had an all-male staff of reporters. It wouldn't hurt to try applying for a reportorial job. The *Bulletin* was easy to locate. Housed in a Quonset hut, it was reminiscent of the kind of housing that belonged to the liberation forces of the US military. Even the edifice's painting was authentic, olive green.

Climbing the stairway to the editorial office, Lor asked for the paper's editor-in-chief, H. Ford Wilkins. She had heard of the paper's strict requirements, how everyone who sought reportorial jobs would need to go through the proverbial grind. Meeting Mr. Wilkins without an appointment embarrassed Lor when Susie Aunario, the senior librarian, asked if she had an appointment or not. She didn't.

But Mr. Wilkins seemed friendly. He approached Lor and offered her a chair across his desk. The usual queries arrived on the scene. He asked Lor about a portfolio. She had none but informed him she could put together clippings from her campus writing contributions. She also did think of her pieces published by the Philippine Military Academy's special issue. Those were recent enough outside from her campus contributions.

"Can you give me a description of your writing experience?" Mr. Wilkins inquired.

"Sir, my writing has been limited to pieces for our campus publication, *The Collegian*. One has to be elected to represent this particular college. In my case, it was the College of Liberal Arts and Sciences."

The editor next asked, "Do you type? How fast?"

Lor answered, "I do. But I don't know my speed. I have been used to a typewriter since I was a first-year high school student. I was a reporter for my freshman class. Truth to tell, I'd rather type what I plan to write instead of writing longhand. It is trying."

"Would you sit by this desk and write some six hundred words about what you think of this office building?"

Lor complied. She started to type. In a little close to an hour's time, she submitted her essay, remembering how World War II came to an end when her hometown saw the US forces build Quonset huts all over Baguio.

> This Quonset building takes me back to the city of Baguio, my most-loved hometown. As soon as my parents felt the excitement of liberation, as America promised, each time they tuned in to shortwave radios, large construction projects called Quonset huts came up. We who watched the American soldiers work were informed that they were setting up those huts. We wondered how fast their buildings would be completed. Those same structures were converted to offices. As we watched furniture transported from numerous trucks to the Quonset huts, we again marveled at the speed by which the work was achieved. The American military started to distribute chocolate bars to us as we watched the construction process. The chocolates that were so popular were Hershey's and Milky Way. There were canned fruits too. I recall peaches, pineapples, and cherries. The Quonset hut that now houses this newspaper publication stands as a symbol of liberation that came to Filipinos. Just remembering the

many Quonset huts built in my old hometown is true nostalgia. I will never forget what a Quonset hut represented, a dwelling that drew expressions of thankfulness for civilians like us. We felt free from invaders. Liberation became ours. We were teenagers whom our elders constantly reminded to keep on praying so we would forget those dark days of enemy occupation. Today, as I write in a Quonset hut, I do remember that a Quonset hut represented so much to numbers of us who never lost hope. A building we had seen built in our midst sprung among us, providing us with the faith that was deeply entrenched in us during the four-year period when the country was cruelly invaded. Not only did a Quonset hut revive our dream of returning to stability, we would no longer have fear in us. As I conclude, I hope this same Quonset hut that now houses the Manila Daily Bulletin, which has a birth date of 1900, will continue to remind the population that it joined construction projects for rehabilitation and reconstruction not only tangibly, but the spirit that was so badly severed was rehabilitated in a war-torn country.

Lor looked over her essay and handed it to Mr. Wilkins. He scanned it quickly. He was quiet. Then he turned to Lor. "When can you report to work?"

"As soon as possible, when I will put together the portfolio you asked me to bring."

"That portfolio would no longer be necessary. We need a reporter on beat. How about tomorrow? I will be here at noon and let you know what areas to cover. In the meantime, I will accompany you to the business office where our treasurer will provide you with the necessary forms to complete. Do you have any questions?"

Lor proceeded to the treasurer's office as the editor walked a few steps behind her. Having completed filling up the employment papers, replete with her school records, she knew she had found the job she had looked forward to. Saturdays were non-working days.

As long as she would cover the beat assigned to her and write the respective stories, a workday would be over. Before she was on her way out, Mr. Wilkins gave her a preview of a work schedule. He gave what Lor would remember always, "short, newsy, straight to the point" news stories.

He commented, "No editorializing. Opinions of the writer don't belong to news stories."

She never forgot what stories she had to write, feature stories from the Manila International Airport, Civil Aeronautics Administration, the office of the Philippine vice president, a few government corporations, and whatever the "desk" would assign to her. Those offices represented her regular beat.

1949 would conclude very soon. Lor would report after lunch to the newspaper office as required, unless informed otherwise. As she was armed with her devotion to writing and the initial excitement that bylines gave her, for the longest time, any story carrying her byline was an exclusive. Inspiration continued to build her confidence.

Her third week on the job saw Lor assigned to interview the first Japanese guest of the local YWCA, Yori Yamamoto, her country's national secretary. After establishing an appointment with her at the Shellbourne Hotel, Lor was more than delighted to meet with the English-speaking YWCA representative.

Japan's YWCA secretary was a fluent speaker who informed Lor how, as a college student in America, she was caught by World War II in her junior year as an international relations major on the Berkeley campus of the University of California. With other co-nationals, as soon as the war was officially terminated, she went home and joined the faculty of a well-known school of religion. Lor learned that Yori had to stay with her church hosts during the war and could not move around without her US guardians.

When Yori learned what took place in the Philippines during those war-torn years, all traced to her countrymen's occupation of the country, she did not hesitate at all to tell Lor how saddened she was. She asked Lor to pray with her so the relations between their home countries would be restored. Yori related how one waiter at the hotel where she was billeted was indifferent to her.

"I completely understand that waiter's position. I waited for my order. It didn't come at all. I thought he was off his shift. So I approached another waiter, who apologized for him. He told me he looked at me as an enemy. I learned that first waiter was the only survivor of his family when their neighborhood was burned down."

Lor informed Yori it was only 1949. The scars from the war that came to an end in 1945 when the occupation troops were defeated would not go away. Both realized it would be unfair to conclude the interview based on memories left by the war. They hugged one another. The interview was ended. Lor promised Yori she would look her up when she would visit Japan.

Returning to her typewriter at the office, Lor started her story. The Yori interview experience highly moved her. Mr. Wilkins thanked Lor for her work.

As post-writing periods went, Lor would go home each evening close to midnight, which was early for her. Whenever she could, she'd catch up to hear the earliest mass at Quiapo church at four o'clock in the morning.

As soon as she arrived home each single day, she would run to the mailbox to look for mail. She saw three pieces of mail on November 12. One from Ermin was clearly identifiable as it was larger than the two others. It was an invitation to attend their academy's Hundredth Night prior to their annual Christmas break for 1949.

A short note was attached, "I would really be very happy if you can attend the occasion, the Hundredth Night. Our class has prepared well for the event. The lower classmen will be participants as well."

Lor thought it wasn't going to be difficult to make a short trip home. She could take the last flight out of Manila on Friday evening because she had no special assignment and could report back to work Sunday without missing a beat.

Never having attended an occasion titled in that manner, Lor was curious to attend it. She pondered, "Would it refer to Shakespeare's *Twelfth Night?*" Scheduled on a Saturday evening, it meant taking a short but invigorating visit to her home. She could return to work via the earliest business flight the next day, Sunday. Also, it was the first time she would be headed home after she had landed that reportorial job at the *Bulletin*. Her parents would not consider it unusual for her to spend Friday and Saturday evenings because they were her off days. Besides, since she could afford the plane fare thanks to a paycheck, there was no need for her to ask Mama and Papa for funds.

At first, she wanted to respond to Ermin, to let him know she would make it to his class event. But there just wasn't time to call long-distance as she looked at the clock. It would be easier to just show up at the event since no RSVP was asked.

Lor made the last flight out of the Manila airport. Arriving in Baguio, it wasn't unusual for her to note the temperature change. She purposely didn't ask for help from their family chauffeur to meet her at the Loakan airport because it was way too late.

Cabs were available at that time so she headed home. As soon as she arrived, she found out her only company for the weekend was Rosie, the housekeeper. She informed Lor that her parents left town on a three-day business conference her father was to attend. Her mother, a school principal, had just started her Christmas vacation. Lor was disappointed that she would not be home to greet her parents because she was returning to her job early Sunday, hoping they would understand how a weekend break was all she could get as she had just started work.

Saturday arrived. Lor did not entertain the idea about having to inform anyone at the academy about her plan to attend their event. It wasn't a hop. Following a dress code was unnecessary. Again she looked at the invitation she received. It clearly meant it was an entertainment of sorts, music and comedy.

Lor called cab service so she could go to the academy's social hall. Her parents had the family car. The venue was just five minutes away by cab, and off she went alone. Not one of her friends knew of her presence.

As Lor arrived at the hall's entrance, she was amazed at the large crowd. She presented the invitation, thinking it was required. As she joined the line, there was no indication showing reserved seats, which she felt was just fine. A girlfriend of one of Ermin's classmates called her to join them with other guests who preferred to occupy one of the first five rows closest to the stage.

The event started on time. Curtains covering the stage's entrance were drawn. Lor could not believe whom she saw as the first person in front of the heavy stage curtains. It was Ermin. He was going to be the event's master of ceremonies, according to the programs that were distributed, found on their seats.

Listening to Ermin's opening remarks was a surprise. He seemed extremely at home. He spoke extemporaneously in welcoming the cheering crowd that filled the hall. Thanking those who came from far away, which included parents and kin of the Cadet Corps, Ermin looked sincere and glad to begin the program. Then as he glanced around the rows closest to the stage, he saw Lor and gave his large smile as he went on leading his schoolmates to get ready for their star-studded performance

Despite the large crowd in the hall, it was cold. Lor kept her heavy sweater on, leaving her lighter coat to cushion her seat's back. There were amusing dialogues and conversational quotes that Ermin started to convey to the audience.

Lor was looking directly at the emcee. She perceived he was reading from a copy as he delivered jokes. No, he continued to extemporize. After an hour and a half of song, dance, and drama between laugh-provoking conversations, Ermin announced it was time for the intermission. Coffee and cookies were to be served at a certain section of the hall.

From the stage, he immediately sought Lor where she was still seated.

As Lor extended her hand to accompany her greetings, Ermin grabbed it and said, "Welcome! Thank you for making it. How lovely you look! You are carrying a professional look too! What a pre-Christmas present to see you! I had no inkling of your arrival. Of course, it is so refreshing to see you amidst the audience. I am glad I was able to mail that invitation to you. I didn't know you had joined the *Bulletin*'s reportorial team until I saw one of your bylined stories. That's when I was positive you became a reporter on beat. You never told me you are now a working girl. Well, congratulations! I will be reading that paper more often from now on."

For the first time while in that hall, Lor found herself short of words. How handsome Ermin looked! She could have been her knight and would have not erred at that moment while she quickly uttered a phrase of thanks. She let him know she wouldn't have been at that hall without the invitation received from him.

She told him, "Invariably, I make time to come here. This city will always be home for me."

Ermin begged to be excused. He scampered to the refreshment corner to get Lor what he thought she preferred, remembering she did not drink coffee.

Returning to her seat, as he joined her momentarily, Ermin offered a mug of hot cocoa. She thanked him profusely. She needed that drink. She wondered why she was feeling very cold. The half-hour intermission was over. Ermin returned to the stage. More and more entertainment numbers were announced. Most were satirical, pleasant diversions referring to plebe characters.

Some included focusing sarcastic remarks on their tactical officers who were crudely mentioned. The incidents that kept on entertaining the audience were original plots. Lor did not pay much attention to all the scenes that continued to unfold via song and dance. She gazed at Ermin who, at that time, looked like a natural on the stage for the role he was asked to take over. He had a sense of humor, much like what she had seen of him earlier when they first met. This time, she told herself, he seemed much at home, wearing that unforgettable smile with the gleam in his eyes!

"His handshake was still firm," she told herself.

The program was almost over, as performances' conclusions go. From the stage, Ermin walked fast to enable him to talk to Lor.

She had forgotten to request a cab to take her home. Worry started to come. But Ermin, familiar with the trials that not having cab reservations were likely to cause, joined Lor. He helped her put on her coat and told her it would take a long time for them to hail a cab.

"Why don't I walk you home? If my estimate is on target, it can't be more than a twenty-minute walk. Besides, the healthy and cool air will do us good. It was getting stuffy in the hall."

While still deep in conversation with Lor, some in the audience came up to congratulate Ermin for his work as master of ceremonies. He introduced Lor to whoever approached them. Looking at Lor again, Ermin repeated his suggestion about walking home with her because the line to the phone in the hall to gain cab service was getting longer. Lor didn't object because she knew she'd need to go to sleep in time for the earliest flight to Manila.

Lor noticed Ermin had another coat (also part of his uniform) to keep him warm. Donning it, he indicated he would follow her down the hall's steps to the street below. He extended his gloved hand initially and then removed his gloves so he could walk astride Lor. When he offered his hand, she did not object.

She was really cold. She no longer had the habit of wearing gloves anywhere. Walking hand in hand in the dark and the cold, Ermin asked why she did not respond to the invitation he sent. At first, she felt odd about holding hands, but she welcomed the warmth. For one of the few times in her growing years, she was feeling very, very cold.

"I wasn't certain I could make it. Besides, there wasn't any RSVP. I thought it was just a general one. Had I known of your participation, I would have replied immediately. I enjoyed listening to your emceeing role. I found the audience hugely appreciated your sense of humor. Keep it up!"

"Thank you for your kind remarks. If we didn't have any sense of humor, this world would easily be a dull one. I have always believed in what laughter can do. We can't be serious in having to weigh too many issues. When the right time comes, that's when we need to make decisions wisely because they can be life-changing," Ermin commented.

Their walk was pleasant. Both talked about their World War II experiences. He told Lor how his oldest sibling enlisted while still in school and died in the infamous concentration camp at Capas, Tarlac. She talked about how Baguio had so many Japanese-manned sentries and pointed out familiar certain spots as they hurried through blocks where the soldiers once kept their vigil. The walk was over. It was just as Ermin timed it, not more than twenty minutes.

Lor rang the doorbell. Rosie opened the door. Lor asked her to bring them hot drinks, both coffee and cocoa. The house was warm. Rosie lit the living room's fireplace adequately. Lor and Ermin continued their conversation between sips of their drinks. He had coffee; she had cocoa. The ladyfingers and caramel candies were untouched.

Softly, Ermin placed his hands on Lor's. She did not make an effort to move his hands away. Looking at her firmly, he said, "I don't know whether this is the right time to offer you anything. You are already a professional. I am still on the road to learning. I have chosen to serve in the military. I look at a military career. It will be one of trials and difficulties. We do not choose our assignments. It would be unkind of me to ask you to stay with me wherever I would be assigned. But in my many cherished moments, I have always wanted to have someone in my life like you. I don't have much to offer except myself.

"As soon as our class graduates in 1951, you will be way ahead in what you are doing. Will you join me as a team, if you will be looking at a change in our civil status, in looking forward to something we might be able to put together? It is not too early to profess our commitment to one another. I know saying it now is rather early, but it is timely. When does it ever become that right time when it comes? There's always love in this proposed togetherness. I did admire you immediately after our first conversation. I wasn't lovestruck. You are my rarity. Love isn't premised on romance alone.

"Romance is part of it. Of course I do feel very romantic, especially now that we can look at one another just like this. I would like to take you in my arms. But that wouldn't be right. You're here in your home without guardians. I don't want to take advantage of you. I'm looking at the bigger picture. Of tomorrow. Of many such tomorrows.

"When we first met, I knew you were the object of admiration from some of those who met you much earlier before I did. I was curious. They had mentioned your writing prowess, saying you were only in your last semester's freshman year when you were elected as the college representative to **The Collegian.** *That's* impressive. It was the first time I saw your name on your university publication. I picked out your school paper from our campus exchange publications. I did send the same request to other female writers on the paper's masthead. I had also learned how you were the object of attention, yes, affection too, from your old university campus friends.

"When I saw you the first time, I waited before I could approach you. You looked happy with your college group. I had known you were not going with anyone. Knowing you did not have a steady was a source of comfort for me. I looked at you physically from a distance. This is the closest we've been since.

"I won't even say it was love at first sight. It was the other way around. Subtle attraction from a distance? Whatever attempts I had at communicating with you were brief. But I was able to know you better with every reply I received from you. Time is golden during our study periods. Your letters were gems of wisdom to me. I'd read them not only once, but thrice.

"All lights are off at ten in the evening. We rise early. Ours is a life that runs on schedule. Much as I wanted to keep on corresponding with you, I had to find the time. You haven't heard much from me. Nor I from you. Whatever I tried to do were short attempts. But they were always done in absolute sincerity. I hope you read behind the simplicity of what I sent you as presents.

"Will you join me in my quest for commitment? I won't pretend that I was never at all attracted to girls. I've known and corresponded with at least eight coeds too. I did believe I thought I was in love, only to fall out of love fast. That's why I haven't used the term 'love.' It seems to be overused.

It occurred to me, if processed in that manner, love isn't what it is. It looks like a physical attraction, too short to think about. It's markedly different the way I feel for you. I admire you for what you are. I love you."

He wrapped her hands in his and kissed them very softly.

Lor didn't know what to say. She had heard him. She pondered, "Had I fallen in love too? Was what I heard from him love?" He was defining love in terms of commitment. But she couldn't return any kind of commitment because she had no idea what it was all about. Already, she had plans for her immediate future.

"I have one request," she heard as he spoke slowly, continuing to gaze at her. "When I was here during your party last year, I heard some dance music. There was a jitterbug piece. May I hear that same music if we could use your portable stereo?"

Lor played the Glenn Miller version of "In the Mood." He rose as he put his arms around her back and asked her to dance. Surprise was hers. She had never seen Ermin dance. But he did. He could boogie. It wasn't bad at all.

Then another Glenn Miller request followed, "Moonlight Serenade." This time, he danced as closely as she sang a few measures. He didn't know Lor had a great singing voice.

"Another surprise," Ermin said. He replayed the same piece.

No words were exchanged. He held her tightly, dancing closer than the first dance, as though he would never release her. Then both dancers heard the living room clock strike midnight. It had been close to two hours since the Hundredth Night was over.

"When do you need to report back?" she inquired.

She heard him say it was understood that they couldn't get back to their barracks at Camp Allen because they had to escort guests and cab transportation was difficult to have without confirmed reservations after socials.

With Rosie's help, Lor inquired from the lone cab service (whose phone number Rosie had memorized) about the availability of cab transportation. It would take another hour. Ermin started to put on his coat. He informed Lor it would be a shorter walk back to their barracks.

Before he left, he thanked her for her hospitality, held both of her hands tightly, and kissed her forehead lightly as he brushed away her bangs. Lor arranged his coat's collar. A button needed adjustment.

Then he was off. He did not see her tears as she closed the door, seeing him hurry back, walking briskly as he was on his way out. Lor resented why she didn't tell him how she felt, that she did love him back. There was just no one like him at all. How she so wanted to let him know! But she didn't.

"That time will still need to come," she assured herself.

Lor got on her flight as scheduled on Sunday. She slept on the one-hour flight because of her inability to sleep the night before or whatever was left of it. From the airport, she went directly to the *Bulletin* office as though the past weekend's schedule of Friday and Saturday did not happen. It looked like a dream, as though she was just on a short assignment.

1949 was over before Lor knew it. There was no word from Ermin. She knew he was to return to the academy after the New Year holidays, after spending the long-wished-for vacation with his family.

Lor went on schedule with her 1950 calendar. She was busy. Aside from her reportorial job, other publication editors asked her to write on feature stories, and the editors called her pieces on exploratory writing as "fabulous." Lor also wrote book reviews for *Freedom Magazine*.

1950 came. Lor's employment at the *Bulletin* now gave her the privilege of a fifteen-day paid vacation. It was time to see that particular vacation fulfilled. No other choice was there but home. And it was summer too. It meant more friends from Manila would be going to Baguio, the summer capital. Those friends wanted to see more of Baguio, which they failed to visit earlier. As close as they had become in college, they asked to view the Philippine Military Academy.

Lor informed them that the academy was in the midst of a physical move to its new home, Fort del Pilar near the Baguio airport, outside the city per se. But she did add the information that the cadets were at their summer camp in the Polo Fields area (within the city) and would be off to their new home after the summer.

In the midst of their sightseeing tours, one friend asked Lor to go to the cadets' summer camp. She was glad to do just that. They proceeded to Polo Fields. A group of Ermin's classmates was at the visitors' site. Lor asked them to give her friends a tour. They obliged. As soon as their tour was done, Ermin, who also had company, saw Lor and her guests at another tent site for tour guides, which included him.

on my account. Before I delve any further, let me tell you that my decision to let you have the fullest essence of emancipation and freedom is not tempered by hearsay, which has been coming my way of late. Neither is it because I have no regard of what has transpired all along. I am not going to take back what I have told you in my initial attempts at delineation. They remain unaltered. Because of my desire to see you exercise your own mind in the way you deem best, without me in the way, I am giving you up. A number of people asked me to clarify their speculations, and I, in turn, changed the stem of queries to your side. Perhaps by their linking you to me, it affects your relationships with others in more ways than one. Verily I do not want this to occur since I would never forgive myself if I stood as a deterrent to one's happiness. I do not like you to lose your chances with other members of our feminine world. I have no right to be that mean by lessening your intrinsic values. I have been deliberating over this issue even before I came up. I firmly believe that, no matter what a girl does to a man, if he does not stick to her, she will never be able to hold him. Before this wedge digs deeply, I have to resort to this. I understand very clearly how anyone would like to exercise his very freedom in every sense of the word. As I have previously stated, I do not want to act as an obstacle in this regard. It is very much better this way for both of us. In the recent past, I acted only in deference to your wishes. If you will recall your own words (and I used these very words as gauges to my conduct toward you), I believed you were strictly on the level with me as you reiterated. So just like a chapter from Life's Book, I had my foretaste of so many novel things. Love moves in a mysterious way, its wonders to perform. Yes, to everyone there is a first time, and I had my share too. You said that keeping that thing unaltered as the years pile on depends on both parties concerned. I suppose I was not rendering the fullest justice due you, and I tried to make amends. But then the best I could make of the situation remains a conundrum. For you, it must have been a glimpse such as tourists usually meet, a glimpse flashed and taken into the heart and flashed once again. You are not to blame for this. This is only living true to being a species of homo sapiens. There has never been a satisfactory explanation for the attraction of two people who don't know anything about each other, drawn together as if by invisible strings. But is love ever final and complete to a woman as it is to a man? Men store their affairs like paid bills in designated compartments of their desks. And while a love affair to a man may have a definite beginning and a middle, a woman rarely thinks of it as being over, however little love is left that continues to flow with time. Suppose this might have been no more than an amusing little game, a finished unit, a paid bill pigeonholed forever? This I leave to the confines of your own conscience and mine too. I have to be emphatic about one thing. I am not disappointed in love. I will never be. It has brought me true values of numerous doings. It is only the realization that it has been such an easy mark that rankles. Strive as we may with the present, it is constantly being destroyed even in its moments of realization as we build moment by moment, living only on an infinitely formal point of time and consciousness. Moment by moment as we live and build, the life and the structure of those moments are swept into a past that is recoverable and tenable only through the medium of memory. We have no home in the present because it is too fleeting, vanishing segment by segment as it comes with incalculable swiftness. We have equally no home in the future because the future is a vast, mysterious, and unpredictable complex of chance combinations. Any accident of fate, any slight interference of our own will, and the whole kaleidoscope of possible destinies shifts in a bewildering haze of possibilities.

Our real home is in the past, in the silent place of memory in itself a shadow and ourselves but shadows moving amid the uncertain ghosts of imperfectly remembered events. There, I am sorry I have done some perambulating at your expense. I have no intention of infringing on your more important tasks and pursuits. Before I say "let's part as friends" (and good friends too), let me tell you how thankful my heart is to you in so many ways—for giving me an insight of one of life's most wonderful feelings; for going out of your way for my sake; for letting me see how men are in their veritable shades and tints; for being a pal and a friend, making me share my unspoken thoughts with you; and for being you. May you always look aloft for heavenly guidance and fortitude. Remember that you have in me a friend who wishes you the best of everything in life for all time.

Lor concluded the letter, ***"Most sincerely."*** She did not read her letter over. She admitted that she could not trust herself. She might delete some parts that didn't sound fair. Yet she wanted it sent as quickly as possible. Tomorrow could hardly wait.

As soon as she sealed the envelope, it was ready for mailing. She went to bed undisturbed. She told herself she felt lighter because she had told Ermin what they had between them (if any, she queried herself) was over and done with.

The next morning, she requested a change in her return flight to Manila. She was glad there was no extra fee she had to come across with because there were many chance passengers similar to her status. The counter clerk noted her ID and informed her that members of the press were given courtesy about flight changes because of the nature of their profession.

Although she did not have to report to work immediately because there was a four-day period left on her vacation, Lor went to the *Bulletin* after she dropped her suitcase at home. A half-dozen letters were awaiting her at her suburban Manila family residence. But there was only one from Ermin. An envelope showed three postcards, all dated close to one another in dates. The cards showed three units of the armed forces, the way Ermin described his early summer visits to her.

There was a letter enclosed:

> I had you always in mind when I visited those units because I imagined myself in one of them as we would plan our future together. I have not made up my mind which branch of the service I would be seeking a notch in. I will ask you to help me when that time comes, most likely a few months before graduation in early 1951.

There was no mention at all of Ermin ever receiving Lor's last letter during that latest home vacation.

Lor's first impulse when she would receive any mail was to respond. This time, she didn't. The final letter she mailed to Ermin on her last night home would speak for her. No further word was required. It must have been received in twenty-four hours. In fact, she was confident he already did receive it.

Work beckoned. It was mid-1950. Clearly it became much easier for Lor to face her writing assignments. Her official news sources were very cooperative.

She would occasionally be assigned to sub when the regular reporter on beat would be unavailable. She considered it a treat to sub, particularly on the defense beat, which had the best and, in her opinion, the most honest news source.

The defense boss, Secretary Ramon Magsaysay, was affectionately called "The Guy." He broke the backbone of the local communist movement, the **Hukbalahap.** There was deep discontent springing from the masses that Magsaysay identified with. Ranking high among those issues were graft, corruption, poverty, high illiteracy, malnutrition, and similar problems that had grown exponentially.

As Lor recalled her coverage of The Guy, she hoped that part of her narration wouldn't put her in the genre of name-droppers. She met him in the midst of the life of a reporter on beat, part of the coverage one was inclined to sub when assigned. Lor knew, as staff reporters go, each one is ready in a heartbeat to pinch hit when the regular is unavailable. There were at least four occasions in a row when Lor's assignments became routine. On one of those early out-of-town designations, the defense secretary noticed how Lor was the only woman reporter among the eight others who were regular on the defense beat.

He approached Lor and inquired of her, asking how she became a hard news reporter. Their friendship became cordial when both found out they were both Ilocanos, from northern Philippines, where Ilocano was their common medium of expression. Magsaysay continued to wonder how a young girl like Lor was that brave to join the batch of reporters, to be the only one from her gender too. He asked whether she already had romantic relationships.

When she replied none, the defense secretary started to counsel her. He emphasized how important it was for those from the feminine gender who worked in that field to marry only those who would be superior to them, as he explained what he meant.

"Women should seek men who are their intellectual superiors," was the first bit of Magsaysay advice. "Otherwise, if a woman is more intellectually superior and marries outside her circle, the union won't be happy. There will be problems. No marriage will last with those problems."

On another occasion when Lor subbed, Magsaysay inquired again about whether or not she already had a boyfriend. Lor told him she didn't. The Guy informed her he was going to volunteer to be her firstborn's godfather if the child would be a boy.

1951 came. There was absolutely no word from Ermin. That convinced Lor he did abide by her May 1950 letter. In the meantime, she was informed by the graduate schools where she had applied that the earliest openings would be in the fall of 1952. There were no other qualifications to comply with. Lor's choice came as she had hoped. She was admitted as a Barbour Scholar to the University of Michigan. She would be informed about student stipends and other scholarship benefits available to international graduate students.

What interested Lor, highly aside from her benefits at Ann Arbor, was one that would see to her transportation back and forth, the Fulbright Scholarship. She was going to save her salary from then on until her departure for the United States. The future was looking brighter with each passing day.

Before her next birthday anniversary on August 19, her present arrived in the form of a letter from the Department of Foreign Affairs, informing her she had passed the first foreign service examinations, which meant she would qualify for a posting abroad.

A letter for Lor from the Office of the Defense Secretary arrived at the *Bulletin* in mid-January. It had a special note attached to a graduation invitation. The defense secretary was invited to serve as guest speaker during the commencement exercises of the first postwar class of the Philippine Military Academy on February 17, 1951:

> Since you are from Baguio, you probably might want to see your home despite the brevity of the coverage. It will be a late morning session. We should all be able to make it back before the day's end. There will be a short reception.

The class is less than seventy. Therefore, the distribution of diplomas won't take that long.

For the first time in months, Lor cried. "If only I could," she told herself. But she knew she could not maintain an attitude of calmness by joining the defense secretary's trip and going amidst the graduating class, stating her congratulatory wishes to those she knew personally. Lor immediately responded to the secretary's aide and informed him she would be sending a letter to Mr. Magsaysay.

Lor was convinced it would be a wonderful opportunity to see those she had known well among members of the class of 1951. But what stopped her was the very thought that she would definitely run into Ermin. Maybe he already had a girlfriend. She learned of an event, the Ring Hop, in late January 1951 that focused on the graduating class members and their partners, those who slipped on their class rings. She just could not bear the thought of seeing Ermin again since May 1950.

As soon as she had collected her thoughts, Lor wrote a personal letter to the defense chief:

> Someday when the opportune time comes, I'll tell you why I won't be able to join you as you generously invited me to attend the Philippine Military Academy commencement exercises.

Life went on for Lor as 1951 sped away. She had a savings account tucked away, as she did plan all for her graduate work for the school term of 1952. She continued to contribute to other publications in her spare time. Meanwhile, she became an active member of the Manila Newspaperwomen's Association (MANEC) and started to join the National Press Club (NPC) as well. She returned to dancing at the NPC with a few of her co-newsmen. But their thoughts were not in sync with hers.

Everyone seemed to be content with what they were doing as news reporters. Nobody ever mentioned further studies abroad. Everyone seemed truly happy. Some told her they led separate lives from their spouses. Divorce was not legal in the Philippines.

"We consider ourselves single," some of the male reporters said.

Her colleagues at MANEC treated Lor as a younger sister. They too gave her pieces of counseling.

By Thanksgiving 1951, Lor stopped looking for mail. There was nothing interesting in her office's mailbox. What made her look at something was an envelope that had the same return address as the stationery that used to come from Ermin's class and himself too. The letter writer was one of their former math professors on the teaching force of the academy. Earlier Lor learned he was a widower, bringing up three of their children. Not one was ten years old. Lor felt slighted.

She pondered, "How could that professor ever think of writing to me, asking permission to visit me in Manila, and asking to call on me, should I be at home in Baguio? A widower? Did he think I was going to acquiesce to his requests?"

Lor slowly felt indignant. She cut up his letter, accompanied by his Thanksgiving greeting card, and threw it in the trash bin. She resolved not to reply to it at all.

Christmas came and went. Time just melted away. 1952's signs were starting to descend on the mountain city. It was exactly the way Lor had known home. Lor felt she would be free, maintaining her schedule up in Baguio because she no longer would have visits nor information about and from the class of 1951. As she wandered about her city's Session Road, she felt nostalgic all of a sudden as she heard band music that accompanied the oft-heard "Baguio Cadets" parade, part of the Sunday presentation of the academy.

The corps proceeded to the Burnham Park grounds, where their buses awaited them for their return to Del Pilar Heights. Invariably it was a sight for Baguio folks and out-of-town tourists to see the academy cadets march the way they did. As soon as she got back home, Lor turned to her old phonograph and tuned in on her favorites. "There Must Be a Way," was the first record. She was going to change it, but decided to continue listening to it:

> There must be a way to make me forget that we're through. There must be a way to make me stop loving you. There must be a star in the skies that isn't reflecting your eyes. I just don't know how to disguise how much I miss you. There must be a kiss to give me a thrill like you do. I looked for a way to be happy, happy with somebody new. Oh, there must be a way, but I can't find the way without you.

Again Lor couldn't cease crying. She repeated the song and sang along with it. Ermin once heard her sing another song when he visited her at her Manila residence in 1949, and he had given the record to her as a present. Lor almost forgot its name. But she remembered, "The Sunshine of Your Smile." He told her he always was more interested in words than music, remembering the first song he alluded to, "Because of You."

She looked for "The Sunshine of Your Smile" among her stack of records, thinking she could have thrown it away. Lor saw it was still there with its wrapper because she didn't want to throw the latter away.

It had a couple sentences from Ermin, "I wish I knew the composers of these melodies. But I am far from being a musician. I am not familiar with this song's melody. I just love the lyrics."

Lor played the record. She listened to it very carefully.

> Dear face that holds so sweet a smile for me.
> Were you not mine, how dark the world would
> be. I know no light above that could replace
> love's radiant sunshine on your dear, dear face.
> Give me your smile, the love light in your eyes.
> Life could not hold a fairer paradise. Give me
> the right to love you all the while. My world
> forever, the sunshine of your smile.

Lor burst into sobs. It was no longer just tears. She really wondered about the non-communication. It was close to two years. She wondered, "What happened? Why didn't he sound off at least during the holidays? How about phone calls? Not a single, solitary way of communicating. Was he married?"

Lor knew four of Ermin's classmates got married on graduation day in 1951. She received three invitations, but she knew she couldn't go to any of the receptions because she was afraid of running into Ermin. That much she knew and admitted to herself.

The next day was her last weekend free from her regular shift. She was in Baguio on assignment. It was the New Year. 1952 arrived. As Baguio did serve as a vacationing spot, the managing editor told her to see some government offices at work, those whose headquarters were in Manila, for example, the Supreme Court and the Court of Appeals. Was there anything newsworthy from those offices?

It was a short break. But she welcomed it. She knew Baguio would bring a number of memories. But she was glad she didn't have to go to Fort del Pilar, the last home of the class of 1951. She had no desire to see it. Another ten-day vacation at home was truly a welcome one.

As soon as she arrived in Manila, she reported to her office, where she found a handwritten memo from Mr. Wilkins. It detailed her next assignment. On January 23, 1952, she was to go to the Vicente Luna General Hospital, where she was to interview the first Filipino released prisoner of the Korean War. If all would be ready, her editor would be back early afternoon, and he would send a photographer to the site. It was only ten in the morning on January 23, 1952. She thought it was too early to go to the hospital for an interview. It was just another job.

Arriving at the clearance desk, Lor showed her press ID. The guard informed her she needed to get more security clearance from the medical officer-in-charge (press relations), whose office was in the next building. Lor felt she was being pushed around. None of her previous assignments ever asked for more clearance. But then those weren't security-bound, like having to interview a former prisoner of war still in his isolated cell for medical reasons, she cautioned herself.

As instructed, she went to the second floor of the building where the clearance could be availed of. She was informed the officer was in conference and would return after lunch.

"Gee," she told herself, "it's only fifteen minutes after ten. It would be a long wait."

Lor decided to plan what to resort to in the event someone else could provide her with the clearance because it was still early for lunch. She had to fulfill her assignment. She had just made the stairway when she heard a chorus of voices. They emanated from a line of officers. They were taking their physical examination for 1952. After all, the year had just started. That was how physicals were administered.

She looked around. She was the only one in the crowd who looked like she didn't belong among the officers awaiting their turn, alphabetically arranged, as she saw the alphabet series flashed by a hospital nurse.

"Hello, how are you?" Lor heard a louder than usual greeting.

She looked at the greeter. To her indescribable surprise, it was Ermin. Still standing, unsure where to take her seat, Ermin pulled a chair and placed it beside the couch where other officers seemed to be awaiting their turns. Lor hesitated. She didn't know what to say.

Seeing her discomfort, Ermin moved her chair away from the couch. He carried another chair closer to Lor's and walked briskly to the Coca-Cola machine, where he retrieved a bottle of the cold drink. He then handed it to her. Again he eyed her very carefully. It was close to two years since he had looked at her, astonished to see her face-to-face. She looked just as astonished.

"Well," she heard Ermin tell her in a much lower tone. "Are you looking for someone in this physical examination department? May I be of help?"

Lor explained why she was at the military hospital, as quickly as she could relate her quest for information that day. She related how she had to see a certain medical officer for release, but he was not available. The physician-in-charge would be one to determine the clearance in terms of interviewing the former war prisoner. Again Lor felt she had nothing more to convey. She was embarrassed.

Ermin was back to his old self, smiling. And as expected, he extended his hand again. She took it, unaware she was sweating and could not understand why all of a sudden she had nothing to say. For one of the isolated moments in her reportorial life, Lor felt so awkward.

Ermin recounted how he had followed her almost three-year life as a newspaperwoman, lauding her for her well-crafted news stories and letting her know too that he had read a couple or so of her feature stories in the *Sunday Times Magazine* and the *Saturday Mirror Magazine*. He congratulated her for her professional work, changing his tone as fast as he could.

"Why have you never replied to my letters sent during the close to two-year period since I last saw you?"

Looking up at him, Lor inquired, "Where did you address those letters to?"

He replied, "Where else but to your Manila home address."

"I don't live in Manila. We have a family residence in Quezon City. You must have had the wrong address. Didn't you visit me once at that Heroes Hills address?"

Ermin pulled out a small directory from his pocket and pointed out an address he claimed he had been directing his letters to. It was Lor's residence all right. He corrected himself, "What I meant as Manila was another one that wasn't Baguio. After all Quezon City is contiguous to Manila."

Then she ventured a reply, "If you knew where I work, why didn't you send your letters to my office address? Most everyone knows the location of the *Manila Daily Bulletin*.

"I don't write to friends at work. I prefer contacting them at their residences."

Glancing at the hall room's clock, Ermin moved closer to Lor, and he almost couldn't be heard when he asked, "Can't we start all over again?"

Lor didn't know what to say. "What was he referring to?" she thought to herself. And she knew "all over again" was what she clearly heard.

"Lor, you know how I've felt for you. I've loved you from day one. I don't have to repeat it. I told you in my letters that I was getting close to finishing my education at the academy, which was just the beginning. There would still be postgraduate courses in the military, possibly abroad, should I qualify. And our assignments are never known until we receive our orders. I've said all these in my letters to you. It is obvious that what I did express to you didn't sink in, did they? I never heard from you at all. Definitely no response to any of my letters. None," he stated empathically.

It was Lor's turn to respond, "I've been busy too, applying for scholarships in the United States. And I have just been accepted for the fall 1952 session, aside from having landed an assignment in the foreign service. So far, things have been looking well because all I need to do is first prepare for the scholarship musts and report in July this year for orientation. If I wish to finish the master's program I applied for, I can complete requirements in less than four semesters by attending one summer session, being ready to submit my thesis before the summer."

Lor's plans took Ermin by surprise. "In other words, you are not intending to start all over again with me, as I repeat it? I had informed you all about those plans in the last two years, but I never heard from you. I went through early 1951 with rituals at the academy. Do you know I was the only one in my class who didn't go through the Ring Hop? I slipped my own ring away from the Ring. Everyone had partners. I asked you to join me. No answer came. I felt so alone. Then there were the commencement exercises for us, the first post-World War II graduates of the academy. I sent you an invitation too. I also sent you a photo. Again I didn't get any response. Do you know who our commencement speaker was? The Honorable Secretary of National Defense. He has been bruited about as the next president of our republic. We have cheered that news, and we hope he does accept the candidacy. We need someone like him to spearhead our campaign against communism."

Returning to a more serious tone as he continued to speak, Ermin said, "Since both of us are still free, why don't we get back to one another, forget about your plans for this year, and get married? I know you've always wanted to be a Valentine's Day bride. We can do it. February 14 is three weeks away. I can manage a simple military wedding at Camp Crame chapel. I belong to the Philippine Constabulary, by the way. Didn't I tell you that, as soon as assignments came after we received our ranks as eager second lieutenants, my assignment was and still is detachment commander, 8th Battalion Combat Team, Second Military Area?"

Lor was stunned. Again she could not respond at all. All things she was hearing were unknowns. She was getting so confused.

Finally, a nurse announced the arrival of Major Belisario. Lor approached him and asked for the needed clearance.

Lor once more extended her hand to Ermin, but he hugged her instead. He walked with her to the building exit. He told her he had never forgotten how he loved her and whispered he still did love her. He said she never looked lovelier and couldn't tell her enough how her presence enlivened him. How he did miss hearing from her touched her tremendously.

On the way to her interview, Lor's eyes welled. She had to stop at a drinking fountain. She said a short prayer so she would be capable of asking the right questions to be directed to the subject of her interview. Lor was fearful she might break down.

The last hour was way too much for her. Fortunately, the interview went well. She had forgotten her stage fright. She felt her subject was at home with her after her discovery. Like her, he was Ilocano too. It was easier to talk to him.

It took a couple hours before Lor could return calmly to the *Bulletin*. She proceeded directly to her typewriter without greeting anyone at the office. It was so unlike her not to say a word at all to anyone when invariably she'd join her colleagues for snacks after her return from an assignment.

Typing away providentially, Lor finished her story as quickly as she could. Tears were rolling down her cheeks. Her typewriter keys were getting soaked. Getting up, she placed her story on Mr. Wilkins' desk. He was away. He had not returned from a late lunch.

Returning to her desk, Lor placed her head on her typewriter as she cried further. Susie, the senior librarian, heard her muted sobs and hurried over to Lor. She then asked what the grieving was all about.

"Were you victimized by a pickpocket? Did you lose your wallet? Was there a death in the family?"

Lor's other office mates, noting what was happening, rushed to Lor's desk. They tried to comfort her. A pitcher of cold water and a beverage glass were placed conveniently to allow Lor to speak. But she had no answers. She tried to evade their questions while her sobbing continued. Finally someone suggested how everyone in the group should go to the visitor's room for privacy's sake. Lor followed them.

Slowly between sobs, Lor narrated what had taken place earlier. Tessie, one of her listeners, grabbed the phone closest to the room and called the military hospital. Speaking quickly, Tessie asked Lor to write down the name for her.

After reaching the appropriate office, Tessie was glad to learn that the candidates for the physical examination had to return the next day because the x-ray machine was out of order.

To be certain, suggestions came from the anxious listeners to find out whether or not Ermin was on the return list. Finally Tessie showed relief. The query drew a positive answer. Ermin was one of those on the schedule: 11:00 a.m., January 24, 1952.

All of Lor's listeners were unanimous in their decision. They wanted her to return to the hospital the next day to enable her to talk to Ermin longer. Everyone agreed it was the best she could do for herself and her future, although they all knew where she was headed that year, academically and professionally.

Lor did not really know what to do next. It was unusually early for her to return home after a working day. But since she was done with her assignment, she didn't want to hang around the office any longer. She needed to think hard. She needed strength.

On her way home, Lor passed by the Church of the Black Nazarene in Quiapo where the most intense devotions had just taken place on January 9. The number of devotees was unparalleled when it came to those who faithfully assembled each time the feast took place.

Praying longer and harder than usual, Lor thought deeply about the collective advice of her office pals. She recognized she was in a daze. She decided to go home.

As soon as she arrived at her residence, she locked herself in her room. She thought, "Am I going to heed the advice of my pals at work?" She thought of the one that was underscored by them. She had to see and talk to Ermin again the next day.

Remembering the initial conversation about correspondence she had with Ermin, Lor decided to inquire from Patria, their helper who had been with the family for fourteen years. Patria was at her usual spot, folding table linen pieces, ready to put them away.

Nobody else was home. Lor's four other siblings were in school. That gave Lor considerable confidence in her planned queries directed to the correspondence and other forms of mail that she was going to seek from Patria.

Although Lor was the second-oldest child, she was the only one who had finished college. Her eldest sibling had two double major studies in the field of music, which took longer time.

Cautiously Lor asked Patria about letters and all kinds of correspondence addressed to her. Patria did not hesitate to inform her how Mama had directed that all letters with the return address of the Philippine Military Academy and those clearly identifiable as male were to be discarded.

Patria took Lor's hand and led her to the garage's only room, reserved for empty large suitcases and similar items that had to be stored. In one move, hidden behind boxes that looked unimportant, Patria handed a dusty sack to her.

Looking at the sack's contents as quickly as she could, Lor pulled out letters that were addressed to her in Ermin's familiar handwriting. She saw a whole stack of them. Two items stood out, thicker than the others.

Hastily, she opened them. One was an invitation for her to slip on his ring at the traditional Ring Hop at the academy in January 1951. The other was a similar invitation in February 1951 to attend their class' commencement exercises, the very first one to take place after World War II.

Hastily she opened the rest of the letters, arranged them per postal date, gathered them, and carried them to her bedroom. There were twenty-six items. A response to her last letter to him that 1950 summer in Baguio was there. Like all the others, that particular one was unknown to her. She read it. Then she reread it. Ermin refused to abide by her terms.

Although she might give him up, he didn't feel that way. He would always be there for her. Nobody else could be the object of his affection. No, he was not going to be stopped in his tracks. He would continue to keep in touch with her.

"Was that asking too much?" was one of his queries.

Interestingly, she saw other letters from her old campus friends.

Giving Ermin's mail another once-over, Lor reread the two larger envelopes that she had read earlier, two invitations for separate events, both that took place in the earliest months of 1951.

"Nobody else is going to slip my ring on me but you," a note attached to the Ring Hop invitation said. A photo of Ermin was likewise enclosed.

The invitation to their class' graduation bore the same anticipation, and another photo accompanied it. Lor couldn't stop her tears. How could she have been denied those letters?

As a writer, she felt her liberty and self-expression were taken away. How could that ever be possible when she was close to twenty-one years, when she would be a legal adult in August 1952? Ironically, she told herself, she who was championing the causes of freedom, liberty, and dignity were taken away. Would she now be getting out of a two-year captivity?

Sarcastically, Lor told herself that she would inquire from Mama as soon as she could. But then, she contradicted herself, that plan might not work out. It would not change what did take place already for close to two years.

Also Lor felt she would not disclose the truth about the fate that befell Ermin's letters. What if they would eventually get married? Would they start life laced with grudges and hatred for what did take place because of Mama's decision? Of her strict orders that no mail from male writers be given to Lor?

Then and there, she had digested many of Ermin's letters' contents. She made a major decision. She would return to the hospital the next day.

Lor stopped crying. She told herself she had no reason to hide her feelings. But she was determined not to tell

Ermin about his letters that she had never seen in close to two years.

She still had one opportunity to clear the air. She'd bring up the issue of nonreceipt of letters addressed to their home when her father would likewise be around, not just directed to her mother. Her *Bulletin* pals were correct. She needed to talk further with Ermin.

Gathering her emotional strength, after she reiterated her appreciation to Patria, Lor asked for supper. Her appetite was back. She could not believe she had skipped food all day.

Waking up comfortably early, Lor called a cab service and went directly to the military hospital. And sure enough, the officers were there. They were in line, in the same manner she had seen them the day before.

Ermin was the tallest among those close to the end of the line. He saw Lor immediately and fell out of the line as he directed a request to the nurse he'd return when his time came.

He immediately noticed Lor's discomfort. "Do you have an answer for me?" he asked as he approached her as quickly as he could.

Instead of articulating any response, Lor pointed at the vacant chairs. Ermin understood her answer. She sat and looked at Ermin in deep earnest, recalling what had been taken up the day before.

"I have analyzed what we discussed yesterday. Yes, I accept your proposal. We can get married in two years, the same day as we did discuss. I believe I can be back from graduate school and complete what shall be required of me.

I'll give up seeking a foreign assignment." Lor was certain she was blushing. She felt extremely warm despite the cold air-conditioning.

She heard him as he remarked, "If we don't start all over again very soon, we will lose each other once more. You have been unheard from for close to two years." Turning to the nurse who was prompting the calls for the officers' turns in an alphabetical order, Ermin requested, "When it will be my turn, please let the others go ahead. I don't mind being the last for the other set of the required physicals."

Returning his gaze on Lor, continuing what he had to say very softly so others in the large reception room wouldn't hear him, Ermin said, "Lor, you know how I've felt for you. I've loved you since day one. There is no need to repeat it. I told you in my letters that I was getting close to finishing my military education at the academy. A bachelor of science was just the start. There would be postgraduate courses still in the pursuit of a service career, possibly abroad, were I to qualify. And our assignments would never be known until we receive our orders. I've disclosed all these in my letters to you. It's obvious that what I did express in writing to you didn't sink in, did they? I never heard from you at all. Definitely no response to any of my letters. None."

Quickly he brought out the two extra important dates to him in 1951, the Ring Hop and Commencement Day. Lor was silent. She could not tell him how she found out about those occasions only through reading his letters hours ago.

Yet she felt it was her turn to respond, "I've been busy, applying for scholarships in the United States. And I have just been accepted for the fall 1952 session, aside from having landed an assignment in the foreign service, which I just told you about earlier as I joined you in this room. So far, things have been looking well because all I need to do is prepare for the scholarship musts and report in July for orientation. If I wish to finish the master's program I applied for earlier, I can complete requirements in less than four semesters by attending one full-time summer session, being ready to submit my thesis before the beginning of a new semester."

Ermin was once again taken by surprise, "In other words, you are not intending to start all over again with me, as I've reiterated it? I did inform you all about pre-graduation ceremonies in my last two years at the academy. There was no word from you at all. But I continued to write. I went through early 1951 with the rituals our school go through. One is the Ring Hop. Do you know I was the only one in my class who didn't go through the January Ring Hop? I slipped my own ring away from the Ring. Everyone had partners. When I didn't hear from you, I sent you a letter and my photo. I informed you there would be nobody else who would share the Ring Hop event but you. The date was held. I was by myself. I never felt so alone. I never heard from you at all."

Before Lor could elaborate on an answer, Ermin continued to describe his pent-up feelings as he placed his hand on her shoulder, "It was with humble pride that I was a member of that well-publicized graduation ceremony of the first post-World War II graduates of the nation's military academy. I sent you an invitation likewise, accompanied by my photo. Again I didn't receive any response. I'm certain you know who our commencement speaker was. The Honorable Secretary of National Defense. He has been bruited about as the next president of our republic. We have cheered that news, and we hope he does accept the candidacy. We need him to spearhead our campaign against communism.

"When I didn't hear from you, I told myself you must have known about our graduation before the date itself. I don't know whether you understood what I was already trying to bring up yesterday. Marriage cannot be postponed. We must stay together. I cannot see you doing what you decided to do, get married, and go to school somewhere else. And I'd be somewhere else too.

"What kind of marriage are you describing? I know you are ambitious. I know you want to achieve your academic dreams. Your desire is to move ahead the way you've planned it, education wise. That's not how I look at marriage. Marriage means physical togetherness, planning more of a future together as the days go on, and making life-changing decisions. In the future, you can always go for more schooling when I will be with you.

"I was so exuberant yesterday when I saw you again. But I cannot accept what you have just told me. It looks like you don't mind absence at all. How can mutual planning ever take place when there is physical absence? Your ideas do not jibe with mine. That is not how I look at marriage. I will repeat: marriage includes physical togetherness and more.

"There, I have underscored physical togetherness. It seems you have not taken this phase into consideration. Marriage to a member of the military cannot be compared to civilian life. I chose it for my career, to serve God and country. That's the reason why I strove to finish the four-year course to the best of my ability—my devotion to duty and my faith in the profession. When I met you, with the wealth of understanding that you shared with me about life and how the future would take care of itself through commitment and devotion, I knew I had found someone who would not hesitate to share life with me. This is still how I feel at this moment as I am explaining my insights to you.

"We are both Leo-born, horoscope wise. Perhaps this did not occur to you. Joking aside, the common knowledge is that partners in marriage should not share the same horoscope. On the contrary, I believe in sharing and understanding one another. I don't believe at all that there is anything wrong in having the same comprehension of horoscopes. Instead of conflict, I believe there is greater understanding. But before going any farther, I have not heard you say you return my love and affection for you. I must hear you say it," he said in a serious tone.

Lor immediately responded in whispers, "I do love you, Ermin. I've told you how in so many of my letters. Do you think I would have returned here today? It took considerable guts for me to come here to enable me to see you again, after close to two years when there wasn't any word received at all from you. Yes, after two long years. I didn't have the sheerest idea where I could reach you after yesterday. Had I failed to see you today, here at this same place, I would have sounded off to our defense reporter for an SOS. He would know what to do, or maybe I would have called on the National Bureau of Investigation to help. I've covered that office too."

In a flash, Oro pulled out his wallet, exposing a closely folded item that looked odd. It was strange and faded. Its edges were almost torn. He held it up. He asked Lor to make a guess. She couldn't. Oro opened up the item.

Lor guessed, "Is it a document? Pages that are part of a collection? An old order?"

"Why did it look that way?" she asked herself. She had never seen anything like it. She started to touch it. But he prevented her from proceeding.

As he held up the item, he said, "You might have thought that, because of this, this would terminate a relationship. Dead. Or to be emphatic, died naturally. Buried, not to be revived at all. Wrong. I didn't. Something like this cannot terminate one's feelings."

Lor's curiosity persisted. Gazing at Ermin's right hand as he started to unfold the worn-out item, she extended her hand to receive it. Ermin opened the item very carefully, placing it on the table between them. Still Lor couldn't figure it out. Then she looked at it more closely. It was a typewritten item. It didn't look professionally typed.

As they faced each other, she could not make out anything at all. "Why would you keep something like that?" she queried.

"I did. Because it is mine. It is the only one that shows somebody really cared for me. It is an original. Someone truly valued me. Someone tried to say it but couldn't directly state it. Read it. You might be able to comprehend it."

She stretched out her hands, afraid the item was going to be further damaged. As soon as she saw the first page, she recognized it, her letter of May 4, 1950. She read it over. She recalled how she didn't review it. She remembered how fast she sealed the letter so it could be sent out to its recipient as fast as mail could run.

As Lor looked down, reading more on the second page, she started to cry. She drew her handbag that lay on the table as she searched for her handkerchief. Ermin came to her rescue and handed out his own hankie.

"This should help you out. Your tiny ones won't work," he said.

"I have never seen you in tears. You look human now. Go ahead. Don't stop yourself. It's going to help you if you cry." He got up and patted her head.

Lor couldn't stop crying at all. The others in the room looked at her cautiously.

"Let's go back to our conversation. Shall I go ahead and ask my parents to come as soon as possible so they can ask for your hand? Are you together with me in my plan? That we get married on February 14? On January 27, I will go to our headquarters to submit the request for permission to marry. Like all documents, it will take time to go through steps. When I get the required approval, it will enable me to make arrangements at the Catholic chapel.

"Both of us have to apply for a marriage license. I have inquired. We can get it anywhere, in Manila or Quezon City. I have asked my brother to look around for a sensible, affordable two-bedroom apartment.

"I have thought of a short visit to Hong Kong. Do you have a valid passport? I am good for four days in that Crown Colony. I asked my brother to book plane reservations on February 15. We'll stay four days at the Peninsula Hotel in Kowloon. A simple reception after the church rites is planned at the brand-new Bay View Hotel's Lotus Room on Dewey Boulevard. Ours, as I indicated earlier, will be a very simple military wedding. Organ music is available according to the chaplain. Are there any details you wish done? Church decorations? Rings?"

Lor was speechless. She knew she would need to tell her parents. The idea broached to her by Ermin was not what her mother had dreamt of. As the first one to get married in her family, her mother had a lavish wedding in mind, inviting at least two hundred guests from both sides of the family. After all, in the Philippines, the groom always bore the financial side of any wedding. But Lor would go ahead. She was never for wedding pomp. If her mother would oppose their plan, as Ermin pointed out, she would not alter it at all.

Ermin continued to talk, "I don't know why there was too much silence from you. Not a word. I wrote you faithfully for two years. I mentioned how I would wait for you if you weren't ready to settle down. I was ready emotionally. My hopes rose when I learned you were not anybody's girlfriend. It meant so much to me. When I first saw you at that 1948 hop, I told myself I would get to know you better. Already I had my idea about who would be the mother of my children. That's how much I thought of you then. You kept on dancing, and I didn't ask to dance with you because I wasn't a good dancer. Remember, we had just two dances together at your home after our Hundredth Night of 1949. Do you still have memories of that evening? After 1948, I joined the dance club at the academy. I learned to dance those very dances I saw you enjoy. Now I think we can dance as long as we can if you will accept my offer of marriage.

"Now that we are face-to-face with one another, I have become firmer in my convictions. At twenty-six, one has learned a great deal about life. I know I am much older than you are, but you are so emotionally mature. So wise. You have held yourself. You don't know what seeing you again meant to me. I really thought you had accepted someone else's marriage proposal. But if you did, I'm certain I would have heard of it. That was my consolation. You didn't accept any of my classmates who pursued you in their own manner.

"Is there anything you wish to take up? I'm certain you know what a second lieutenant makes. Two hundred fifty pesos a month. If he gets a foreign assignment, overseas compensation is attached. I won't ask how much you are making if you wish to continue working. I can't make you stop because you love your profession. It's up to you.

"I told you I would be going back to the battalion functions as a detachment commander. Since you are off early on Fridays, maybe once every two weeks you can leave on the last train for Lucena. I'll meet you at the train station, and you can leave early on Sundays to allow you to report to work. I'll do the same every two weeks so we can be together as much as possible.

"I see a medic approaching us. Maybe he is being sent to fetch me to enable me to finish the physical exams. If you wish, we can walk back to the building, if it doesn't take that long. I can ride back with you if you'll be returning to work at this time."

Lor didn't realize it was Ermin who was doing all the talking while she listened. What was occupying her now were details. She had to prepare her wedding ensemble, inform Mr. Wilkins what she planned to do, and tell her parents about her plans. She was never for big weddings. If her mother did not side with Ermin's decision, she would abide by Ermin's wishes. They would simply go ahead. She would tell her mother it was not an elopement. She was getting married properly with scant trimmings. But it would be a church wedding.

She went back to the building with Ermin. The physical exam didn't take that long because almost all of the officers who had lined up earlier had left. The nurse understood what she had to do when Ermin asked to use the phone, to call a taxi. In Ermin's company, they hailed a cab. On the way to her office, Lor informed him they should both proceed to Manila's city hall, where they would apply for a marriage license.

The clerk at the window for marriage license applications told them they needed to present documents. The most important ones each one would present was the original birth certificate. If not available, a certified copy would do. There was a waiting period of at least ten days.

That meant nothing earlier than February 10, 1952. It would be too late for Ermin to contact the chaplain of the military chapel chosen for the wedding's venue. Likewise, he needed to procure the approval of the permission-to-marry application required of graduates of the Philippine Military Academy before they could get married.

It was time to go home. The next day, both Lor and Ermin decided to meet again at the city hall, where they presented the required documents. Fortunately, Lor had kept her birth certificate at work, inside her locked office desk. Ermin had his too in the briefcase he carried. But both Lor and Ermin thought the ten-day waiting period was too long. Ermin needed the marriage license before he could confirm use of the military chapel in line with the chaplain's instructions.

Lor had an idea. She knew whom to contact. She phoned Dave Miguel, the *Bulletin* reporter who covered city hall, often seen at the mayor's press office. Dave knew the rounds. Lor presented her press ID at the office of Manila Mayor Arsenio Lacson. Fortunately Dave was there.

Explaining their situation, Dave went to Mayor Lacson himself, who called the chief of the marriage license bureau to take care of Lor and Ermin, informing the chief that Lor was a member of the press and a colleague of Dave and Ermin was a graduate of the military academy. They were informed the license would be ready in an hour. It was safely in Ermin's briefcase. More errands awaited both of them.

February 3 arrived. Ermin accompanied Lor to the *Bulletin*, where he met Lor's closest friends. They were impressed that both Lor and Ermin had made plans in that short time.

Now it was their time to do what they could. Ermin left Lor at her office so he could contact the chapel's chaplain. He also had to present the permission-to-marry approval certificate, the must for all academy graduates before they could apply for marriage. There was also the need to apply for a short vacation.

In the company of Dita Aviado-Roseburg, an advertising manager of the paper, Lor went to a couturier specializing in wedding gowns. Each one among her close friends volunteered to give what was needed. Details on the wedding ensemble per se were taken care of in two hours, and the entire outfit would be ready in six working days.

Lor didn't want to try on the dress until the real day, so she asked Luz Bertha Angeles, a sorority sister, one of her college chums who had the same measurements, to don the gown. Another close friend informed Lor she would take care of the floral decorations in church. One who had the same shoe size offered to lend something borrowed and something blue. The bouquet was prepared in the same manner all the wearable items were done, with maximum use of hearts and flowers. Each friend who offered to help informed Lor not to worry about payments. The items represented their presents to her. She was not to spend a centavo. All chums had one desire, for Lor to start off on the right foot because they knew she was going ahead without her family's knowledge.

After covering her beat for two days, the next day, February 5, Lor waited for Ermin, who passed for her at the office. They had their first dinner alone together. It was at a restaurant of her choice in a Manila suburb, the

D & E restaurant. She asked the waiter to light the table candle, the very first experience she had having dinner with someone other than the usual bright lights. She had read about the pluses of romantic glow. Little wonder the candlelight evoked privacy.

Ermin moved closer to her as he took her left hand and kissed it. In a minute, he brought out what was a ring measuring rod, letting her know they would need to go out to the jewelry shop to select their wedding rings. But it would not hurt to know her ring size so the jeweler would narrow down the choices to what was available within short notice.

Looking at her timepiece, Lor knew it wasn't time to return home. It was her turn to talk, to make Ermin listen to her. She knew he covered a lot of ground. But she wanted to find out, reporter that she was, about certain matters.

"Who was with you when I saw you in May 1950 at Polo Fields? I saw a group of older girls who wanted you back with them when you did notice our group with your classmates. Was anyone among them a girlfriend? What was her name? I had never seen anyone of them at all at any of your events. Of course, I cannot claim to have attended more than three of your academy-sponsored occasions."

Ermin tried to remember the incident. He laughed. "Are you showing you are capable of jealousy? It is a good sign you do care. There were six visitors at that same summer camp tent. Three were daughters of a retired military officer, and I don't know the three others who were in their company. Yes, they were guests of one of our tactical (tac) officers, married to the tallest girl in the crowd. The other two were our tac's sisters-in-law, who were on the quest for graduates-to-be, meaning members of our class. I wasn't interested in anyone at all. They never finished college.

"Do you think, had they been my personal guests, I would have left them the way I did when I saw you with my classmates and your friends? I was surprised to see you at summer camp at Polo Fields. But you left as fast as you could, and that was a disappointment. You acted as though I was just a mere acquaintance. I was hurt.

"Let's not go through what took place two years ago. It's not worth our time. We have to talk about the next few days so we can acquire the wherewithal to exchange marriage vows. I overheard your friends at work, all excited about helping out. They don't need to do that. I have some savings so I can pay for expenses, like Filipino bridegrooms do. It's up to you to proceed. But please let them know you are the bride-to-be and you have a ready, willing, and able groom."

Lor took time to absorb their conversation. She informed Ermin she would proceed in the manner he had outlined details to her. Before the evening was over, although Ermin suggested he would escort her home, she could not be brave enough to face the music because she knew she would need to see her mother. She didn't want to accost Mama about those letters Ermin had no knowledge of. Lor wanted Ermin to see her family the way he had heard of them.

"If Mama were to see me with him tonight, I don't know how I would handle it," she cautioned herself.

"Let's not involve Mama yet. If you take me home, she'll want to know why we are together. You haven't met her formally at all. All she remembers is having met members of your class and you were among them. She would not recall one from another. Over time, she says, 'They are all in uniform. Can't tell one from the other.' "Papa is in Baguio." Let's wait for him to make it back here so we can save time," said Lor, trying to be as tranquil as she could.

"It's up to you, Miss Arce," Ermin said. "Let me see you off in a cab, and I'll be on my way. Incidentally my parents will be arriving in a few days' time. I will let you know where and when we should all meet."

Lor took the cab and headed home. She started to mark her calendar as soon as she got to her room. Indeed it was February 5, 1952. They had just a few more days to go to put things together. February 14, 1952, fell on a Thursday. That meant she had barely nine days. No one in her household knew of her plans. Yet she never led anyone to suspect there was something different.

Jotting down "must matters," she remembered what Ermin told her about what was already taken care of from his end. His parents were arriving on Saturday, February 9. Lor had already been given a week off from work, but she preferred to go on with her beat, to keep her from worrying about being around the Sunday date of February 11 when Ermin scheduled the meeting with his parents and Lor's. The huge concern was Lor's papa. He had postponed his trip to Quezon City, and there was no exact date of his arrival.

As she looked at what paperwork was completed in reference to the wedding, Lor heaved a sigh of relief. Ermin reassured her he was ready. So was Lor. Her wedding ensemble was finished earlier than anticipated.

Saturday, February 10, arrived. Ermin called Lor at home, asking when their parents could meet. Lor had no answer. Her father was still in Baguio. The next day, Lor went off to church and informed Ermin where it would be easier for her to meet his parents. She would need to explain to them that her mother was the only parent at home and it was extremely important that both her parents should meet with Ermin's parents.

Ermin informed Lor where they could all meet. His brother had already made arrangements regarding the reception venue. He told her a Sunday lunch at the Bay View Hotel restaurant's Golden Lotus Room would be their meeting place.

Reporting early to work at her office, Lor finished a story she was to conclude as an investigative report, about the waterfront, an assignment she loved each time she was sent to cover potential anomalies.

Arriving in a cab, Lor went straight to the restaurant where Ermin and his parents were awaiting her. Ermin gave her a brief hug, kissed her on both cheeks, and held her hands firmly as he introduced Lor to his parents. He told Lor she was to address his mother as "Inang" and his father as "Tatang."

"Both accents on the last syllable." He smiled.

Ermin knew Lor was not at all fluent in Tagalog, the national language. Both came from opposite sides of the country—she from Northern Luzon and he from Southern Luzon. And as far as they had known one another, both did not deviate at all from their common medium, English.

Ermin's dad asked a few questions as he led off the conversation. He talked about how pleased he was to learn that Ermin was going to have a wife who came from the same university campus where he worked for his degree as an English major.

Inang, as Ermin addressed her, spoke in Tagalog. She informed Lor how she did not finish school. "In my time, we could do what we wished to do if we didn't feel like attending school. I now regret that, but I've tried to help myself by understanding English and reading newspapers in English."

There were more subjects to discuss. They spoke about how they wanted to help both Lor and Ermin to start off. They informed Lor that part of that day's agenda was to meet their close family in the Manila area. They also wanted to see the apartment they were going to have as their first home.

Lunch was served. Lor was really hungry. But she seemed she could not eat. Events were folding out so swiftly. She could hardly believe what was taking place. In a few days, she would be married. The issue she had entertained about Papa's absence was taken up by Ermin's parents, who insisted they wanted to ask for her hand. Lor told them about praying he would be back before February 14. She added that it would not aid their cause if her father would not be there with her mother when they would all meet.

The afternoon was spent in meeting Ermin's first cousins. There was the Leelin family, sons and daughters of the only sister of Inang. And there was the Tancioco family of her only brother, Eduardo. Ermin's first cousins, Lor learned, were all still in school. He also asked all his younger siblings and one older sibling and his wife to be at their residence that evening. They were all surprised to learn how fast the decision to make Valentine's Day the wedding date of Lor and Ermin.

Lor told them how and why Valentine's Day was her choice. She narrated how her mother, a school principal, would react at the conclusion of each February 14. Some of her co-teachers would be happy; others were in tears because their respective husbands or fiancés would not remember them.

"I told my mother that would not have happened to them had they gotten married on Valentine's Day, which nobody would ever forget."

Laughter filled their atmosphere as Lor related what she knew since. "I made the announcement to my mother. I was then in the seventh grade. If I were to get married, I would have no other date but Valentine's Day."

At the conclusion of an early dinner held at her sister's residence, Ermin's mother suggested they drop by the apartment chosen for their first home. It was a two-floor triplex. The unit was the end unit facing D. Tuason Avenue in Quezon City. Ermin handed Lor a key before he opened the main door.

To Lor's great surprise, the apartment was furnished. Inang informed Lor those furniture pieces represented their presents to them. Lor hugged them both, thanking them profusely for their generous thoughtfulness.

As the three spoke in Tagalog, Ermin's mother took Lor aside and told her she did hear of her when Ermin was still at the academy.

"I asked Ermin for your picture so we'd know how you look like, but it seems all he had was an old photo, one that accompanied one of your articles that he told us about, and that was what he called 'your meeting.' I see you still have that same hairdo."

February 12, 1952, came. There was no word yet about Lor's papa. Lor greatly wished to make a phone call to find out when he was expected, and she prayed he would at least make it on or before February 14. That same day, she went through her list again. Ermin informed her he had moved some of his personal items to the apartment and a suitcase was ready for their wedding trip. He reminded her she should be as ready because they were to leave for the earliest flight to the Crown Colony of Hong Kong on February 15. Likewise, he said it was going to be a good idea if he would have her passport in the briefcase he always carried for security reasons.

She changed her mind about giving her papa a phone call. Lor assured herself that her father always was around each time Valentine's Day came because he was the first one to greet their mom, who gave that date a sense of significance by reminding her faculty to remember the day.

The big day arrived. A phone call awakened Lor. It was Ermin. He had never called that early. Ermin told Lor that was the last time they would be single. Both laughed. As she listened to him, Lor knew he was keeping his sense of humor intact. Ermin reminded her that he was looking forward to seeing a hyphenated name accompany her bylines. She laughed. But she was starting to get concerned all over again. It was ten in the morning on February 14, 1952. There was no sign of her papa's arrival.

Lor told herself she would be patient. Maybe he would come before noon. At eleven, a call came. Her father called with the information that there was no need for them to send the family car to the airport because he was going to be dropped off by eleven o'clock that same day. His business associate had made pick-up arrangements prior to their departure from Baguio.

Lor was relieved. At last, her chief concern for the day could be threshed out. It was close to noon when she heard her father ascend their house's long stairway. She waited in her room. Her bags were already packed. She was going to get dressed at her wedding sponsor's house near the church. The wedding ensemble's wardrobe items were all ready at the Roseburg residence since February 12. She had not seen the finished product because she was confident Luz Bertha did try the gown on. If it weren't what was conceived, she would have heard her friends complain.

She gave herself one hour before she put on her brave face in her plan to talk to her papa.

Knocking at his room, Lor asked, "May I come in? How was your flight, Papa?"

Lor's father was all smiles as he returned her query.

Lor didn't lose time. "I need to talk to you. I'm getting married today."

Lor's father turned serious. "I didn't know you had a boyfriend. How did this happen? I was gone only a little more than a month, after your last vacation up there. You didn't mention anything at all. Were you that decided then? Why didn't you inform your mother and myself?"

The questions did require answers. Lor told her dad what happened as fast as she could.

He next asked, "Who is he? I don't recall you had given anyone of those academy cadets special attention."

It was Lor's turn to explain further, "You must have seen him in the company of the academy visitors who would come to our Baguio home when I'd be there. Let me go to a specific evening. You had suggested we go to Mansion House [the official residence of the country's president] as soon as the results of the foreign service exams were out. Judge Antonio Quirino knew the Philippine Consulate General in Honolulu needed a press attaché, and he suggested that, since I had the required qualifications, I'd get the assignment through an executive memorandum. That same day, Ermin came to visit because I was to leave for Manila the next day. He came by himself."

"Yes, I recall. There was one tall cadet who came but left after a half hour. He looked very sharp. I noted the disappointment in him when you told him you had to meet a commitment. Is he the one you will be exchanging vows with this evening?" Lor's dad softly inquired.

Lor nodded.

"I remember him very well, although I probably wouldn't be able to place him correctly if he were in a crowd. I recall he had a unique last name. Although he had the cadet's haircut, I could see he had a curly top. I have another question. Do you love him?"

Lor replied, "Yes, I do. I wouldn't be doing what I find myself in now if it were otherwise."

More queries came forth from Lor's father. "Where is the wedding going to take place? Is there a reception? What can I do? Does your mother know? Do any of your siblings know? Where will you live? Will you be joining him at his assignment?"

As soon as Lor gave all the desired responses, tears rolled down her father's cheeks. She had never seen Papa in tears.

"When you were born, I expected a son. I was disappointed when I had another daughter. In so many ways, you made up for my disappointment. I will give you my blessings. I know you wouldn't be proceeding with this decision because you are very intelligent. You have proven how mature you are. How you are able to carry out your responsibilities and professional functions cannot be subject to criticism.

"I know you haven't told your mother about your decision. It must be the same with your siblings. It's too sudden. But you've made your decision. Am I invited to the reception? I'll take care of letting your mother know when she comes home. Use the family car now. Get all the things you need to have in your suitcases. Tell Macario where you need to go."

Running to her room, Lor gathered all her things. Patria cleared her room of what she knew Lor needed immediately and accompanied her to the car, waiting while Macario, the driver, waited for more instructions. Patria joined Lor in the car.

Lor gave Macario the address of her next home. It was a good idea Ermin gave her a key, which was very handy because she gained entrance readily. And because Patria was available, she had ready help to put her things in place.

It was now four thirty. The nuptials were to take place at six punctually. Lor had to go to the Roseburg residence where her attendants were waiting so she could get dressed. It didn't take long for Lor to be fitted in her attire. In the company of Dita, she arrived at the military chapel at five fifty, simultaneously with Ermin in another car that was decorated and clearly seen as a bridal vehicle. His mother rode with him. They entered the side door so Ermin could find himself in front of the altar before the bridal march would commence.

At the chapel's entrance was Colonel Carmelo Z. "Mike" Barbero, whom Lor asked to give her away. She saw all her friends and was gladly surprised that the aisles were tastefully decorated. The hearts and flowers theme was spelled out. Their names were right in the first pews, together with cherubs.

The wedding march's music floated. Lor was amazed at the lovely organ music. She was informed earlier that the organist was the chapel's employee, but the music she heard was just beautiful. Ermin and Lor exchanged their wedding vows. In less than forty minutes, they found themselves congratulated as man and wife.

The chaplain announced, "Ladies and gentlemen, may I present Lieutenant Ermin Oro, and his blooming wife, Lor Arce Oro."

The wedding march was played. It turned out that the organist was Lor's older sister, who insisted she play the very music Lor would have chosen for her day, had she been asked. Lor was surprised when she saw two of her siblings. She was clueless. She guessed her papa must have instructed them to proceed over to the chapel.

With the marriage rites over, the newlyweds were ready to board the bridal car when Ermin's mother strongly suggested they all proceed to Heroes Hills so they could meet Lor's parents. They did. Lor's father joined the group, and as he had assured Lor earlier, he was ready to go to the reception.

Simple music accompanied the equally simple reception. Since it was Thursday, students would still be in school to finish the week. Those who had work commitments to fulfill were ready to call it a night after all the champagne and wine they had drank to wish the newlyweds the best. The guests remarked the dinner menu was terrific. They had lobster and steak. The occasion was a very intimate affair.

After they thanked their guests, Lor and Ermin went to the hotel desk to inquire about their room. They were told it was the honeymoon suite and was paid for in advance anonymously. Both looked at one another, guessing who could be their patron.

Still garbed in their wedding attire, Ermin opened the door to the bridal suite. As he locked the door, he lifted his bride and filled her with the kisses and hugs he had long wanted to give her. He could not stop himself from doing what he had always wished to do since he had known what intimacy and privacy could do for them. Lor looked like a child as he continued to smother her with kisses. He started to undress her.

Stepping out of the shower, Ermin helped put on her robe and picked up a hair dryer as he combed his fingers on her head to dry her hair. She did the same. Drying one another's hair was fun. Lor started to get dressed. As she had buttoned her blouse and slid into her skirt to get ready for their flight, the phone rang.

The waiter informed her that their breakfast was going to be delivered in a few minutes. She conveyed the information to Ermin. He was already dressed, as he prepared his suitcase and double-checked the briefcase's contents. He fetched her suitcase and her train case as if on cue.

Lor was pleased. She did not know that Ermin had ordered room service. It did save them time. There was no need to go to the hotel's dining room where they might run into friends who were not informed they had gotten married.

Looking at the breakfast tray, she saw a newspaper. She leafed through the paper, the *Manila Times* issue of that day, and found their wedding photo. Its caption included a three-column photo accompanying a short write-up, "Manila news hen marries AFP lieutenant."

Lor called it to Ermin's attention, as both continued to read the paper between bites of toast and fruits. Ermin could not believe this was happening. His classmates and friends would know he had finally won Lor's heart, as he noted the item on the page was prominently seen. Lor knew their *Bulletin* photographer, Rudy Sakdalan, was at the wedding. She deduced he must have given the photo to the *Times* society editor, Consuelo Abaya.

Lovingly, Ermin buttered another pastry, this time it was of the sweetened variety, and fed Lor with it. "A few ounces won't hurt you," he said.

He recalled how she got on the scales after he was done with the required physical exam that January 25. "You should put on some weight. You are only ninety-eight pounds, tiny enough for me to put in my pocket," he joked.

They were off to the airport in a half-hour. In flight, they were the subject of smiles and congratulatory wishes as the flight attendant announced, "We have newlyweds who chose Valentine's Day for their wedding day. Please go through today's papers. Join me in extending our best wishes to Lieutenant and Mrs. Ermin Oro."

One passenger stepped up to lead a toast to the brand-new bride and groom. In a brief two-hour flight, the airport of the Crown Colony of Hong Kong was plainly in sight. Lor and Ermin walked to the terminal, where they claimed their checked-in luggage. A limousine driver held a placard with the name, Mr. and Mrs. Ermin Oro. They followed him. The trip to the Peninsula Hotel seemed to be only a hop, a skip, and a jump away.

At the registration desk, the clerk greeted them and gave them their room keys. They proceeded to their room. It wasn't the bridal suite, which made Lor feel better because she was shy about being identified as a bride. On the table was a floral arrangement and a tray of fresh fruits welcoming them. Since Ermin had an activity schedule, he glanced at it and asked Lor to join him in looking at where they would be touring for the next three days.

He was done. The schedule was short. It meant visiting what the Hong Kong side had to offer: a visit to the seafood restaurant erected on the waters and a visit to Macao, another island. They had six hours ahead of them for sightseeing each day. They could look at restaurant menus as they planned to stroll around.

As Lor was changing from her tailored suit to her casual top and slacks, Ermin moved quickly and pulled her to him before she could put on her slacks. "I can never have enough of you." He covered her with kisses and strong hugs before she could finish dressing.

Once more, he told her he could never stop loving her, and she assured him she would do the same forever. They walked from the hotel to the wharf, where they could take a ferry to the Hong Kong side. Before long, they found the floating restaurant they had read about and spent three hours admiring the view around it while indulging in the feast laid before them, generous offerings of crustaceans.

The three days flew by, spent in long walks at shopping areas, parks, and temples that were museum-worthy. Returning to their hotel, Ermin would rush to do what he loved doing in the privacy of their room. He assured himself he could never have enough of his wife. Modest as she was, she no longer hid behind closets to undress herself before going to bed. She gave of herself freely, surprised at her own strong responses as she reciprocated his lovemaking.

Each moment was spent in sheer longing as he guided her patiently, rejoicing in her unmasked giving of herself as she looked forward to every gesture from his lips seeking the ultimate intimacy she was capable of understanding each time they faced each other. Wordlessly. Only their eyes and hugs spoke for the hunger they felt was getting stronger in their faith in one another. They learned to know each other better, emotionally and mentally as well. They did so gradually between shared physical moments of discovery and rediscovery each single day.

They both agreed to short workouts, brief but fast exercise routines in the hotel sports room before they would call it a day prior to returning to their room. They said their prayers together. It made Lor feel secure as she prayed for their future as man and wife.

Each evening after dinner in the calmness of their room, a bottle of wine awaited them. Bedtime was one they both looked forward to. Ermin continued to take his time. They longed for slow, gradual loving. Where he touched, she responded breathlessly. Where he kissed, she kissed him too. He noticed how she was getting stronger and freer in her responses.

Every cell of her body responded to his every touch. The need grew greater as he knew what brought both of them to the heights they desired. Slow loving had its desired outcome. They didn't have to assure one another they belonged to each other as they continued to be one at the end of each day.

February 19, 1952 came. It was the last day of their wedding trip.

"I promise you that we will be back sooner than soon," Ermin said as he started to carry their bags. Before they departed from their room, he kissed Lor with a quick, loving caress.

After their seventy-two hours together, while returning to the Philippines, the four-day Hong Kong visit seemed too short. But Lor and Ermin made the most of their unforgettable trip. They learned a great deal about their insights as they exchanged views on their lines of thinking growing out of the common thread that drew them together, their love for writing.

Their first home was basic for their needs. Ermin returned to his field assignment. Lor did the same.

The month flew by. Ermin phoned Lor and told her he was free during that weekend. She boarded the train in line with his instructions, taking the earliest schedule from the train station in Manila, straight to Lucena where Ermin was waiting for her.

He could hardly wait to help her out with her small weekend case as she took her place beside him in a civilian vehicle driven by one of Ermin's men. It was a short ride. Before they were out of the jeep, Ermin grabbed Lor and kissed her, hugging her close to him, as though he didn't want to let her go at all. They approached the visitor quarters, which was assigned to them. He was overjoyed to see Lor the way she was, still as pretty as he had carried her image in his mind, and lifted her in the room as soon as they had their first private moments.

Ermin learned an inspection of the troops was to take place the next day. He started to explain to Lor that it was nothing special.

Members of HQ's top echelons dropped in unannounced to see how the campaign against the local communists, the Huks, was moving on and how the defense secretary's policy was turning out. It was nothing short of success.

Having covered the defense beat, Lor was not surprised at all to learn how deeply entrenched the campaign had become, slowly winning successfully wherever the enemy was caught. And how her own groom was contributing to that cause made her so proud of him. She thought she saw some familiar faces she had seen at general headquarters when the inspection took place, as viewed from the guest rows. But she never entertained the thought she would approach the top brass on her own. She was there not as a reporter, but as a wife of a member of the military. She remained where guests were seated.

Early Sunday came. Lor took the train back to Manila. She held back her tears as she kissed Ermin "so long." It would be another two or three weeks before they would be together.

With her small train case in hand, Lor proceeded to the *Bulletin* and looked at the notes she left prior to her away trip. She had covered the airport on so many numerous occasions. Since it was a Sunday, she felt it would be nice to see how the airport's renovation efforts were going through. The last time she was on a flight was their wedding trip to Hong Kong.

Instinctively, Lor visited the renovations already undertaken and decided that was to be the next day's story. She did write about what she had seen with more than the usual zest and energy expected of the government's work at refurbishing one of its most crowded venues that controlled both local and international air traffic.

Fortunately, Lor was never alone in their apartment. Her mother-in-law saw to that. Two helpers, Adriana and Aurora, were trained to be on the lookout for Lor when darkness beckoned. Both knew how to maximize public transportation. One Friday evening, because Lor didn't go home straight after work, the two girls fetched her from the *Bulletin*. The three of them had a good time as they dropped by a favorite ice cream parlor where Lor's favorite flavor of the month, a product of Magnolia ice cream, was availed of.

Mondays through Fridays as scheduled workdays weren't that strict on news reporters. That was Lor's good fortune. As long as she covered her beat and wrote her stories, strict schedules were not factored into her employment.

The last week of March 1952 arrived. As she was wont to doing, she proceeded home from her news writing at eight thirty in the evening. It was early enough for her because it was a regular day of coverage on beat. She was not hungry. She had snacked for a long time.

As soon as she arrived home, the kitchen seemed to be alive with more recipes for the three of them. Aurora cooked a familiar dish from their region. Lor asked her why all the extra work when there were lots of leftovers from lunch and she would usually not be that hungry for dinner because of late snacking.

Before she could receive a reply, someone grabbed Lor from behind. The embrace was no one else's than Ermin's. They scampered to their bedroom. No words were spoken as he closed the door securely behind them. Undressing

Lor, he carried her to their bed. She did the same. This time, she had to work faster because he was still in complete military attire, fatigues.

No lengthy conversations took place. Yet Lor wondered why there were more pieces of luggage, boots, and knapsacks on the floor. All the boxes that accompanied Ermin were opened, including the books she had seen at his quarters, thus indicating he practically brought all his personal effects.

"It wasn't just a brief visit," she continued to tell herself.

Before she could ask Ermin, he started to tell her he was given a new assignment to headquarters and he would no longer remain at his first post. Therefore, he teased her, "You need not take the train to Lucena any longer."

When informed about the shift in assignment, Lor inquired why he did not forewarn her so she would have arrived home earlier to welcome him immediately for the first time at their first home likewise.

Ermin informed her it was a sudden decision by his superior officers, who noted he had an extra assignment, that of being a groom to his bride, and there was also an opening for him at headquarters.

As he unpacked his luggage, Ermin brought out a present for Lor, a briefcase replete with her initials, which would come in handy with all her notes, memos, pencils, and pens, including a smaller purse that could fit into the briefcase itself.

Lor thanked him for his thoughtfulness, so very much like the first impression he made on her as she remembered the meaningful and simple presents he gave her during his cadet days at the academy.

Ermin informed her how he was to report to his new assignment the next day. Headquarters was but a hop, a skip, and a jump, he joked. The assignment change made Lor very happy as he joined her on what was now their home front.

It was just the beginning of a workweek, but the change in Lor's schedule was more than just a modification. It was a transformation that meant so much to her. She managed to prepare breakfast for Ermin, and they would have more schedules to share, mealtime wise. He told her how he had looked forward to the new assignment, most likely at a desk, but he'd be able to find out later and let her know the nature of his new job.

Lor joined Ermin in hoping the new job would be to his liking, considering how he didn't have to take care of a detachment like he did for more than two years. She started to prepare a new schedule relevant to running a household. Working on a budget and housekeeping details were now figured out in clarity. Aurora was going to do general housework. Adriana would handle phases of cooking and marketing.

Returning to her beat, Lor felt more at ease because she was confident Ermin was no longer in the detachment that took him to combat duty. Owing to her more flexible schedule as a reporter, Lor told herself she would find time to learn how to prepare simple dishes that both of them relished.

Lor and Ermin's favorite days were Friday and Saturday. The *Bulletin*'s schedule did not include a Sunday issue, which gave reporters free Saturdays. Both welcomed that free weekend, giving them the opportunity to hear Saturday vigil masses. Their early evenings were spent hinging on the movie offerings. Their preferences were identical. They loved dramas on human rights, documentaries, true-to-life stories, and the inspirational.

Months came and went. They found their literary choices jibed with each other's selections. They read to one another. Continuing their love for writing, they contributed pieces on request to publications of their choice.

On their eight-month journey as husband and wife, Lor felt unwell. She sought her primary care physician's help and was informed it was best for her to go for laboratory tests. She did. Her cousin-in-law, Dr. Joaquin Manahan, pathology chief of the Chinese General Hospital in Manila, confirmed why she started to feel the way she did for the first time. Lor was on the way to motherhood in late March 1953. After undergoing tests, her obstetrician/gynecologist assured Lor she was in top health and could continue to resume her reportorial functions.

As soon as the tests were confirmed in writing, coming home from his office, Lor drew Ermin aside and told him they were going to be parents.

He was exuberant. That evening, he insisted on celebrating by going to their favorite dining place. It was the same venue where he presented the wedding rod that sized up their wedding rings.

Lor and Ermin wondered if a larger house were needed. They started their quest almost immediately. In a couple weeks' time, they found a single dwelling that met their needs. An extra bedroom, a third one, was appropriate for one more household assistant.

A few more months came by. Their first wedding anniversary was marked very simply on February 14, 1953.

Lor began to shop around for baby furniture. She delighted in choosing sets of layette for their first heir. Her colleagues suggested neutral colors, like light canary yellow or light shades of green. They hosted baby showers as all of them anxiously awaited the baby's arrival.

In line with her employer's policy, Lor took a brief maternity leave. And a few months later, on April 9, 1953, a national holiday, a son was born to the limitless joy of Lor and Ermin. They named their son Rafael, after Ermin's dad, calling him Ralph for short.

The holiday was to mark the fall of Bataan, one event that continues to be part of history books that recorded valor unsurpassed from the much-acclaimed heroic Death March, when patriotic and courageous allied forces drawn from America's already depleted and vanquished forces were joined by Filipino servicemen who fought to the end against the enemy invaders.

She took on her maternal duties in great stride while a visiting nurse taught her the ABCs of initial motherhood. Consulting Dr. Spock's book formed part of Lor's reading schedule, and she was positive that she did gain tremendous knowledge from that bible of new mothers.

Although away from her regular work scenario as a beat reporter, Lor continued to write and was able to meet feature writing deadlines. Ermin still was assigned to the same outfit he joined after he reported to headquarters after his field assignment.

Lor sensed that, as an intelligence officer, Ermin had several missions, but she never inquired at all about their nature. Intelligence matters were never integral parts of their conversation. Lor was not keen at all in knowing the extent of her husband's knowledge of intelligence work. Each one had her or his duties lined up, which did not conflict with one another.

As parents, in accordance with established rites of their creed, it was time for their son to be baptized. Lor remembered acutely when the then-Defense Secretary Ramon Magsaysay had offered to be the godfather of their firstborn, if the infant were to be a son.

1953 in the Philippines stood out as an era to prepare for the presidential elections, and the Ramon Magsaysay presidential campaign had gone into high gear. He was immersed in nationwide campaigns. Communication seemed impossible at that time. But Lor was not to be daunted. She sent word to the Magsaysay aides.

Having named the date of the baptismal rites the afternoon on June 4, 1953, at three o'clock at Quezon City's Immaculate Heart Church, Lor went ahead and forwarded the information to the aides. She received confirmation of the candidate's presence, but he would be a little late.

Yet shortly after three o'clock that afternoon, that same date, Ramon Magsaysay lived up to his promise. He stood by

Rafael as his godfather, while he joined the other godparent, Mrs. Antonia J. Bengzon, and the officiating parish priest, Reverend Father Ambrosio Manaligod, SVD.

Indeed Magsaysay remembered his promise to a young woman scribe who, at that time the offer to be a godfather was made, had not entertained any thoughts of having a life partner then. Yet years after, Magsaysay fulfilled his word amid the rigid nationwide campaign he likewise had to fulfill among the country's electorate.

As a public servant, Magsaysay accomplished so much in so little time. He was overwhelmingly elected to the presidency. Four years later in 1957, the Philippine nation was immersed in deep mourning when the Magsaysay plane, returning to Manila, crashed on Mount Manunggal in Cebu, Southern Philippines.

That loss was an epic tragedy. Epic because, thus far, not one of those who came after Magsaysay could scarcely match what he did during that short-lived term of his presidency. Tragedy because, based on what Magsaysay accomplished in so little time, he would have done more. And much more, as echoed by those who remember and recall what he had rendered in pursuing what he cherished for his countrymen, without craving neither fame nor fortune.

Even before he was elected to the presidency, when he served as defense secretary, Magsaysay already started to tackle his country's age-old problems, which, to his great credit, he did with tremendous success.

The Guy, as he was fondly called, broke the backbone of the local communist movement, known then as the Hukbalahap campaign. There was deep discontent springing from the masses that he identified with. Ranking high among the issues were graft, corruption, poverty, high illiteracy, malnutrition, and similar major problems that had grown exponentially.

As president, Magsaysay embarked on programs that rendered the country in a laudable position, strong. There were no negative demonstrations at all. Contentment, though modest, was evidenced by the people who worked hard to attain their goals. The Filipino people who followed Magsaysay's route as he shepherded the nation were all in unison when they singled out their leader's attributes, justice and leadership.

That godson President Magsaysay stood for did not veer away from what his sole godfather's credo was, justice. Were The Guy around today, as godfather, he would be happy to know that Rafael, the two-month-old infant he stood for while deep in the midst of a presidential campaign, is a superior court judge of the most populous state of the Union.

1953 wore on. The Korean War continued to become an agenda of the UN. Lor became more aware of the role of the Philippines when word went around that war had not ceased. When Ermin had his orders to join a UN task force, Lor understood that was his duty.

Off to Korea Ermin went. Although he noticed earlier that Lor was pregnant again, as she was having bouts with morning sickness, Ermin did not want her to worry alone. Also she did not wish to tell him until all tests would prove her status. He had to leave within the next few days. The laboratory results would not come on time.

Lor's parents expressed their wishes for their daughter to join them at their family home while Ermin was off on his overseas assignment. Likewise, Lor comprehended the meaning of remaining behind. She continued to be immersed in her writing assignments while she waited for mail from her husband who wrote to her every single day, sending photos of their camp site that spoke loudly—United Nations Commission on Repatriation Group (UNCREG) against the background of deep snow and his uniformed self attired in complete winter gear, showing how winter came to another Asian country, a season that never visited the Philippines.

Lor's second pregnancy was confirmed shortly the day after Ermin's second week in Korea. She informed him about the forthcoming arrival of their second child. Away from home, Ermin had enough to worry about, and since hers was not a first pregnancy, he believed his wife knew how to handle it.

As soon as he received confirmation about another opportunity at fatherhood, Ermin was delighted. He wanted to return home as he did hope he would spend the Christmas holidays with his family. Likewise, he told Lor how he was looking forward to celebrating their second wedding anniversary with another Valentine's Day on the horizon.

Christmas 1954's sights and sounds arrived. Already Lor was getting ready for the season of seasons. As a newspaper reporter, she believed in her heart that the Korean War was coming to an end. However eager Lor was to hear from Ermin, she never pressed him for details. As she prepared for the arrival of their second child, Lor prayed that the conclusion of Ermin's tour of duty would coincide with the holidays.

It wasn't just awaiting the holidays that kept Lor busy. She was deep in writing, zeroing in on her homeland's distinctive mores and traditions observed before and during the holiday season.

Lor's prayers were answered when one day the guest's bell at the gate to her parents' house rang. It was Ermin. He did not let her know in advance about his return. Once more, jubilation joined them. Along with Lor's parents, the entire family expressed thankfulness that Ermin was back, unscathed from a former war zone.

Ermin teased her about her pregnancy. He said she still looked slim, despite the bump that he started to touch as he stated, "I hope our second one will be a daughter."

A daughter it was when April 3, 1954 came. She was named Gilda, after the full name of her father.

Lor and Ermin saw the need of having more room as their family grew. Fortunately, a two-story house was available for a long-term lease, which would accommodate their needs. And with two small children, Lor decided she could not pursue her reportorial commitments. Their household was growing. So were their duties as parents.

Lor looked around for part-time work as a writer. She was lucky she found an opening that did not demand her full-time presence as long as she would do the editorial and writing functions for a monthly publication. Lor worked at home while she could supervise the upbringing of the two young children, Ralph and Gilda. The position she found was just the very one Lor wanted. She fulfilled the duties of an editor, and in addition, she authored articles for the same publication.

1956 was a great year for Lor and Ermin. They were able to purchase a lot that would serve as their future home, thanks to their savings. The next year, another publication asked Lor to do editing functions as well. She took on the additional work because she was certain she would be able to work at home too.

Once more, Christmas was approaching. Lor was carrying another pregnancy, their third child. The baby was expected the first part of 1958 and arrived on the due date, January 9, 1958. She was named Geraldine after St. Gerard, the saint of motherhood.

Lor continued to work on her editing responsibilities for the monthly publication she started at in 1954. She thoroughly enjoyed working as an editor. The fact she was able to combine the functions due her working commitments and motherhood gave her a surge of fulfillment as a homemaker as well.

1959 came. Ermin's assignments were met, more and more missions abroad. Mid-1959 was a competitive year for scholarships away from the Philippines. Scholarships and grants were offered to qualified members of the Philippine military belonging to the Philippine Constabulary, through the Agency of International Development (AID), under the aegis of the US government. With a firm wish to further his studies, Ermin competed. He won the first slot. The primary one was to go for graduate courses offered in Los

Angeles at the University of Southern California (USC) in police management.

The initial agenda included visits to various metropolitan centers in the United States that offered police management seminars. There was likewise a graduate degree offering, a master of science in public administration, which required a two-year stay. Ermin was selected to represent his home country on both opportunities. His wife had to choose between continuing to be a media person or join him.

It was not an easy decision. But she had no choice. Ermin did not wish to leave her behind with three very young kids. He told her he could not go for further schooling without the inspiration that came always from his family. So spring 1960 saw the Oro couple make their first visit to the United States as a family unit.

After touring states away from California, such as Michigan, Maryland, Illinois, New York, Washington, and Vermont, Ermin's schedule was to be spent in Los Angeles, as shown on his orders, so he could work on the graduate degrees. The two-year California stay was dedicated to further schooling.

Ermin's full load in his quest for a master of science in public administration at USC was fulfilled in time. He completed all course requirements, finishing his graduate degree with a straight A, which garnered him the Chancellor's Award. Free tuition costs were likewise part of the scholarship were he to go for a doctoral program.

In the meantime, because USC did not have a graduate school in journalism and communication, Lor enrolled in advanced courses in writing. Through those aforementioned classes, Lor met faculty members who recognized her writing abilities. They encouraged her to apply for the much-coveted status that was in its infant stage. International students who had special gifts and talents would be given the opportunity to return to the United States, based on what they could offer in return to be assets to the country by way of permanent residence, as long as they would not remain continuously in their country of origin beyond eleven months. They would need to renew their status prior to the one-year expiration date granted them.

Lor deeply thought about the feasibility offered by her professors. She did wish to return to USC for advanced degrees. There was nothing to lose. Filling up an application on the recommendation of her professors who were well aware of the quality of her scholastic work would lend the very assistance needed to hurdle the needed visa requirements with the view to be given a green card to allow Lor and her dependents to move freely without restrictions in and out of the United States, in accordance with the law. Following all the instructions, Lor went for required interviews. Little did she think she would have that well-sought green card in a few months' time.

In one of her creative writing classes, Lor had authored one of her on-the-spot feature pieces, which *Ebony*, a national publication, accepted. She had written about a well-known non-professional rider who won several trophies as an equestrian although she scarcely had the training as one. She just loved horses. Horses gave back that love to her.

The accepted piece turned out to be heaven-sent. It was attached to Lor's application for permanent residence, an indicator that she was indeed a professional writer. It boosted her application, according to the scheduled final interview.

May 1962 arrived. It was time for Ermin to return to his military duties. He was informed about graduation day and the honors that the graduate school at USC would accord him. Humbly, Ermin explained his situation to the school administrators. He had to leave at the earliest possible time to allow him to return to his military duties.

The graduate school formally informed Ermin that the commencement program would include his name, according to the committee, regardless of his physical absence. He expressed his gratitude for the committee's generous concern. He had silently hoped Lor's green card might serve its purpose one day. As though she read his mind, Lor informed him he was not included on her application, which had only their three minor children as her dependents.

Leaving sunny LA, Ermin left for San Francisco, where he boarded a military air transport that landed in Pampanga's Clark Air Base, where the United States maintained operations. Lor wanted to visit as many cities in North America on her way back to the homeland. She joined Canada-bound tours and holiday treats in various well-known cities, a treat she enjoyed immensely. Then off to the Far East, she continued on her homebound trip and landed in Hong Kong. In but a short while, Lor would be back to her ancestral home.

As the airplane landed at Manila International Airport, family and old friends filled the welcoming crowd. It looked like Lor had left home for the longest time.

The next day meant getting her family together because of the new school year due in two weeks' time.

Falling in line to pay tuition fees at the treasurer's office, Ateneo de Manila Grade School (AGS), where Ralph was going to be a fourth grader, Lor heard someone addressing her from behind. It was the Reverend Father Luis B. Candelaria, SJ, the AGS headmaster.

After the usual greetings, he asked Lor to join the teaching force, to take care of one of the lower grades. Lor's first impulse was that she thought he was kidding.

"You know I've never been a teacher, Father," Lor replied.

"Of course you are a teacher," the priest answered.

"I don't know anything at all when it comes to classroom teaching," Lor insisted.

"All good mothers make good teachers," the AGS headmaster said. Then he informed Lor how he reviewed her son's standing in class and how he was considered a star student.

"No matter what you've told me, Father, there's just one profession I've dabbled in, writing, my first entrance into the world of journalism as a reporter," Lor responded.

The priest then continued to talk. He informed Lor he was aware of her background after she had completed her bachelor degrees. But he insisted she should try teaching just to prove to herself that she could handle other tasks. Then and there, the headmaster showed a serious mien. He turned to Lor's views as a parent. She responded, saying how she believed in the strengths that the family had developed over time.

The priest commented, "It is only mid-1962. The road ahead for training youngsters in grade school is promising. More and more parents join their households in inculcating their beliefs in teaching them the needed values. The AGS wishes it could accommodate more grade-school student applicants, but it requires not just building expansion but help from the family, the school, and the community."

Returning to Lor, the priest informed her how there would scarcely be time for in-service training, but she would be allowed to write her own lesson plans and handle forty-one third graders by herself. All subjects were to be under her jurisdiction, yes, her guidance, all through her own manner of comprehension in teaching what grade three was all about.

Lor continued to look at the headmaster in disbelief. Here he was back to her, discussing the merits of teaching while reiterating she would take care of a class of third graders. He excused himself and asked her to wait. Then he went on to seek the third-grade head teacher, Mrs. Carmen Gonzalez, an icon in education.

Lor told herself she didn't know any teacher at all in that grade school, let alone those who would be her colleagues, were she to accept the teaching position. Many thoughts besieged Lor's mind. How was she to grapple with the responsibilities of teaching when she had never had any kind of active classroom experience?

Before Lor could mentally review all that had transpired with the headmaster's conversation, he returned with Mrs.

Gonzalez, who discussed in short what grade three was all about. But still Lor had her doubts. She asked the third-grade head teacher to allow some time just for the two of them to get together so she could venture to ask questions relevant to the grade.

They did. Lor was informed she could be given manuals, books, and other teaching aids to take home with her immediately. The cardinal rule was for the teacher to assess the capacity of the class she was assigned to and apply principles of teaching accordingly.

Lor accepted the teaching assignment on one condition, that it was temporary. If she did not fulfill the duties during the initial period, the school would be free to go for a substitute teacher to finish the school year. The two administrators agreed to Lor's conditional acceptance to teach the third grade. In two weeks, school was off to start, she reminded herself.

Her free evenings were devoted in going through all the material she received before the first day of school. Lor read through the third-grade textbooks. One indicated she was going to teach Tagalog, the country's national language, among other subjects she was to handle for the same grade.

She became apprehensive. She was not a native speaker. But she had accepted to teach all the subjects. That was the first challenge she had to meet. As she continued to read all the third-grade requirements, Lor felt less daunted. As she ran through all the titled subject's manual, the methodology seemed readable. It was likened to teaching English: using basic parts of speech and moving on to phrases, sentences, and simple paragraphs, just like any language immersion.

The first several weeks of teaching went on. Her third graders were eager to learn. Lor started with English and Reading, followed by Religion, Mathematics, Writing, and Tagalog. She learned how teaching third graders followed a pattern of zeroing in on some of the usual academically identified weaknesses that seemed initially baffling.

As the quarter progressed, Lor was feeling up to par. She strongly felt she could recognize the students who immediately understood the different parts of speech and how they moved on to writing simple composition with minimum grammatical errors.

A challenge came up during the close of that same quarter. It was the school's tradition to hold quarterly academic contests: elocution both in English and Tagalog and mathematics in English, all to be held in the school's auditorium with members of the same grade and their respective teachers making up the audience, aside from judges in the contest itself.

Lor had scarcely time to prepare her class representatives for that initial competition. Earlier she had zeroed in on seeing to the initial comprehension of her class' grasp of the basic subjects that came within her enumerated functions in the classroom.

Also, as she worked hard on teaching a class, she had to train her contestants. Consequently, her initial efforts were met with success. One of them won the first prize in the English elocution contest. The win made her class extremely proud because everyone considered the prize a feat. Nobody expected her class to run away with the first prize during that initial participation, the very first quarter of the school term's competition. As a consequence, Lor spent more hours after class to train potential contest representatives who had shown their eagerness and enthusiasm to learn more.

Lor held parent-teacher meetings on schedule. She asked parents to uphold the foundation of family values, which their sons would, in due time, make a part of their young lives, although they were but third graders. Also Lor requested parents to join the school's policy in instilling values in line with their sons' comprehension of principles their school adhered to as enhancements derived voluntarily in keeping the family as an institution they cared deeply about.

Each quarter of teaching included participation of Lor's class in the academic contest presentations. Lor continued to train students who would represent the class in all phases that vied for leadership after regular class hours.

Competition in mathematics was depicted through the blackboard. Contestants would show their numerical skills on each blackboard separate from their competitors, where accuracy and speed would be the sole criteria.

Lor chose English speakers extra carefully. She taught them how to enunciate each word and phrase and listened to them at the rear end of the classroom to determine their voice volume and how their actions accompanied the execution of the designated speech piece.

The last and final quarter of the school year finally arrived on the scene. Lor's third graders were adjudged with more first prizes. There was first place in speech. Another took the second place in mathematics. Through the determined efforts of one class participant, he won the first place in spelling. Lor felt proud and humble as she looked back at her initial teaching experience. She thanked the entire class for their cooperation and the manner by which they lent their encouragement to their class contestants as well.

Another challenge came up, written finals for the entire grade. The written finals on all subjects spelled out on the grade's curriculum were to be administered as usual. The outcome was to determine placement of each class member. Those who would do well in the written tests would be moved according to their ratings accordingly. Lor prepared her class to do what each member could render to, not only pass the finals but to do well as each boy progressed with each quarter.

During the last week of that school year of 1962–1963, a messenger was sent to Lor's classroom. She was asked to report to the headmaster's office. Lor wondered what she did wrong. She started to guess. Probably it was time for her to receive her end-of-the-school-year review because, as a new teacher, it was time for the termination of her contract.

On arrival at the office of the headmaster, Reverend Manuel C. Regalado, SJ, he met Lor. He then asked her to take the most comfortable seat and closed his office's door.

Father Regalado didn't lose time in saying his congratulations for a school year's job well done, as he referred to the manner by which Lor's class fared in the third-grade finals administered to all third graders. He told her how her efforts were lauded by the administrators who never received disciplinary reports on any member of her class.

Without looking at written records, the headmaster reiterated his appreciation on Lor's first try at teaching as he indicated how remarkable her efforts in taking care of her third-grade charges proved her tenacity in putting forth the policies of the school. He underscored Lor's abilities in charting her way through the school year, using her own manner of comprehending the needs of her class as the academic contest outcomes and the final test results had illustrated.

The headmaster then changed the subject. He conveyed how the school administration decided that Lor's faculty designation be moved to the seventh grade, the graduating class of the forthcoming school year, 1963–1964. That would be the very first time in the AGS history that the school would have a female member of the faculty assigned to that particular grade.

Lor was speechless. She informed the priest she would be resented by the older students, yes, teenagers who were on their way to high school and beyond, owing to the fact that, as early as the sixth grade, they had all-male teachers.

"No, Father, please," was her muted response. She told him the assignment wouldn't fit her at all. She could not teach Tagalog. Already, she informed him how she had to add extra time for her to study Tagalog while she was teaching the third graders.

In response, the headmaster informed Lor that another teacher, a native Tagalog speaker, would handle the Tagalog class. The seventh grade was going to be departmental. There would be teachers in math, arts, music, physical education, and other subjects that would not be within the realm of homeroom teachers. The course work would entail training student participation in academic contests in the same manner, quarterly, very similar to the methodology observed in the lower grades.

"You won't be the only woman teacher in the seventh grade," the headmaster said. He informed Lor further how the administrators decided there would be two more women teachers in the same grade. The plan would complete their novel change to include seventh-grade women faculty members.

"That step," Father Regalado added, "would be decidedly a first in the school's history."

The priest went on to inform Lor he had designated her to be the faculty adviser for the student paper. In summary, Father Regalado expressed his hopes Lor would accept the assignment to teach seventh grade, as he made it emphatic that it would mark a historical phase for the AGS.

The headmaster continued on an optimistic note about the new change in naming women to the seventh-grade faculty. "In the future, male students will run into women faculty in high school and college. It would certainly be advisable for them to get used to having members of your gender meet them during their last year of grade school as they ascend the educational ladder." He then asked Lor whether she had questions left unanswered.

Lor informed the headmaster how she had certain concerns (not misgivings) about the appointment. Candidly, she stated how she had sensed how boys in their mid or later teens preferred their own gender as their instructors in guiding them to the next step where they could hardly wait to go to college and beyond.

The illustrious headmaster explained that the educational universe was not limited to the masculine world. "If plans would miscarry, change would always be evaluated."

And that was how a first was chronicled in the manner by which the class of AGS 1964 would include women teachers.

Lor felt much better when she learned there would be two other women teachers who would join the seventh-grade faculty. Then and there, she felt it was time for her to respond to the new assignment, as the headmaster disclosed to her as he awaited her answer.

Smiling, Lor graciously accepted her designation, as she expressed great hopes that the student body would welcome the faculty assignment change, not just the seventh graders.

The 1963–1964 school year at AGS commenced in June 1963. Lor's assignment was to teach that graduating class' honors classes with a combined number of ninety-three students.

"Another challenge," Lor told herself.

Along with the two other women teachers assigned to the seventh grade, Lor met the classes they were to handle, representative of their homerooms the first day of school. The boys the three women teachers were to take care of at first looked at them quizzically, according to their male co-faculty colleagues. Having women faculty members in the seventh grade was indeed a departure from the past.

As the school year went on, when asked about the seventh graders' comments, nothing negative was heard nor aired by the students that had women homeroom teachers on the faculty of the graduating class.

Lor was happy to see her youthful students who changed physically also grow mentally and emotionally while they added that sense of maturity that was uniquely theirs. When her homeroom students won top prizes in academic contests, Lor expressed her thankfulness that they responded to the call of class pride and unity.

Meanwhile Ermin's military assignment took him from general headquarters to the Presidential Security Agency (PSA) and the Presidential Guard Battalion (PGB), Malacanang Palace, where he served as deputy director and deputy commander, respectively. At that time, the Philippines had two major political parties. The incumbent president was Diosdado Macapagal.

Lor was grateful that, as an army wife, she knew what was required to earn one's daily bread and butter. (Sometimes, she told herself, it seemed like bread and margarine.) Her gratitude grew because teaching, mentoring, and freelance writing brought fulfillment and pride in contributing to their modest family coffers and professional advancement.

Yet as the months and years went by, Lor could not help but recall the limitless vastness in opportunity and freedom that living in the United States offered as she compared her life in the two milieus: her homeland and America. Keeping in touch with her friends in the States who sent publications and other forms of literature kept the essence of freedom of expression alive.

One morning, close to daybreak in 1965, the phone rang. Lor responded to the call. It was Colonel Ben Tolentino, Ermin's immediate superior. Without saying any amenities, the caller instructed Lor to get the morning papers, loudly telling her to turn to a certain page. She did.

He continued, "Look at the main photo. Why did you pose with the enemy?" Then came the harsh query, "Why are you in the same photo with ladies of the opposing party?"

Lor replied, "Marina Perez, my college chum, wife of Senator Leonie Perez, invited me. She hosted the social, an apolitical gathering of friends. No political affiliations were ever discussed."

The colonel proceeded to berate Lor in disdain, "You joined a picture with the enemy." Referring to Ermin in hostile tones, he declared, "Your presence with the opposing party's ladies was a clear entry on the debit side of the ledger on Ermin's career."

Appalled, Lor countered, "My husband can sail on his own merits. He chose the military for his career. As a graduate of his class' top ten, he can always prove his worth. If fair is fair, his wife could not, should not, and would not stand in his way."

Lor continued to smart under the colonel's statements, "I am not a member of the military. You have no right to upbraid me."

She did not stop herself from telling Ermin's superior that what he just did was plain sexual harassment. Although he had quieted down as she expressed her feelings, Lor asked to be excused from the phone conversation. The caller acquiesced.

Lor had just concluded the summer session as an English language instructor at a private school. As she prepared for her schedule that day, the early morning diatribe failed to leave her. She was enraged. No wife should ever be addressed in that outrageous manner, particularly when coming from her husband's superiors.

"I am not under anyone in the military. Only my husband is in the service," Lor assured herself.

Still bristling, Lor recalled how, in her observations in the United States, a woman was man's equal. Then and there, she made a solemn vow, which she prayed she could keep. That was the first and last time any man would treat her in that manner.

In a heartbeat, Lor decided to return to the United States.

As soon as Ermin was done with his breakfast, she drew him aside and immediately lost no time in describing what took place earlier. He too was enraged and promised Lor he would take up the matter with his boss. But she discouraged him. Instead she immediately informed Ermin what she had in mind.

He weighed their options as he hugged her and whispered, "Go ahead. I will always be with you in whatever you decide to do."

Lor rushed to the US Embassy to take care of the needed paperwork, thanks to the green card. She then waited for Ermin so they could discuss the next moves.

Lor was to leave with the children as soon as they could. Ermin was to take care of leasing out their home. If the price were right, he would sell it. When ready, he would join them in the States.

Lor gathered their children and repeated instructions, reminding them how, in a few weeks' time, they would rely on themselves. No domestic help would await them in their future home. Independently, they would need to make their beds, tidy up their rooms, and do their homework and other concerns that would be theirs and theirs alone.

Their first task was discharged well. They had to determine what they were to carry in but two suitcases each. They chose sensibly.

There was no question about returning to California. The Golden State had served as their residence for two years. Then and there, Ermin and Lor consulted with one another when decision-making time came, zeroing in on those weighty decisions, full of prayer and hope.

The second time around, because of his military commitments, Lor was alone. Ermin could not leave the country. Lor had to be mother and father to their three little ones.

Arriving in California, Lor had three major concerns: locating the neighborhood where it would be safe for their three grade school kids to walk to and fro school; finding housing that accepted small children; and landing a job that would help meet their financial needs (tuition costs and school requirements), augmenting what Ermin could send the family on a regular basis. With much resolve and prayer, the three concerns were met. Friends of old rallied to assist in terms of how to adjust to a new life because of the dual role that was Lor's.

Relatives found out by word of mouth that Lor had returned to the United States without Ermin. They were ambivalent about Lor's decision to be alone until Ermin could join the family. She had to respond to the why each time she was contacted. Lor knew their kin meant well. They had counseled that she should weigh issues well before they could settle down.

Lor's cousins, Consorcia and Frank Sipin, did not hesitate to let Lor know how heavy her burden was as a single parent, even just for a limited period. They invited Lor to move in with them to Watsonville, California, where they lived comfortably. Both wanted to help in bringing up the children. Frank assured Lor there was no need to spend any penny. His was a comfortable position with West Coast Farms, and he promised he would help take care of the children and Lor until Ermin would join them.

Lor thanked her cousins profusely. But she informed them about completing graduate school at USC, where she was admitted to the master's program in journalism and communication, the first time the graduate program was reopened after World War II.

She told her folks she was determined to proceed full-time in seeking her graduate degree, be father and mother to her schoolchildren, and work full-time as she was determined to bring up three children in the chosen milieu.

When the Watts Riots of Los Angeles erupted in August 1965, Lor's cousins strongly insisted that Lor and the children leave the LA area. Again Lor expressed her gratitude for their concern. She told her kin not to worry because their friends who lived nearby had indicated their willingness to help take care of them and protect them to the best of their ability.

Providentially, the Watts Riots ceased. The City of Los Angeles gradually returned to its normal pace. Lor and the three children continued to do what they had planned, to start the fall semester and follow through with their simple agendas.

Full-time work for a university publication as managing editor and senior writer provided a meaningful schedule for Lor as she likewise worked full-time on her graduate course requirements. Despite the load she had to carry, Lor thankfully handled the requirements on time.

Complete cooperation came from the children. Their teachers praised their academic work, calling it "excellent and outstanding." Regretfully, Lor told herself she was unable to spend even a brief study period with each of the children. She was thankful that they managed on their own.

Besides, she had additional jobs on weekends and holidays. She also edited and rehashed papers of graduate students who claimed their skills in the written portion of the English language had much to be desired. Money was not factored into Lor's wish to help the students because they were all professional students and admitted they had limited funds.

Quickly, Lor aspired to be a competent editor to fulfill that part of hers that lay unspoken, her passion for the English language. It was a learning process to correct the graduate students' papers. Lor pointed out their strengths and weaknesses while her editing/writing skills were likewise tested.

As a graduate student herself, she understood what it meant to finish on time. So as Lor and her group of grad students went through the commencement programs, they were happy that they would join the same graduation exercises. No happier batch of graduate school candidates could vie with their group.

Meanwhile, it was time for thanksgiving for Lor and the children. They received word that Ermin was going to join them in America. Initially, they all thought he was taking a vacation. His arrival was happily cheered by the family who had prayed the year's absence from their patriarch would be over, and it was.

Ermin had likewise arrived in time for Lor's commencement. It was Lor's turn to receive her graduate degree as the first and only one who finished in time as the first postwar recipient of the master of arts in journalism and communication at USC.

Eventually, Ermin filed his papers for optional retirement from the Philippine government. With his master of science degree earned earlier at USC in 1962, seeking employment ran a smooth course.

The three children, Ralph, Gilda, and Gerine, pursued their academic work independently while immersed in the requirements that school laid out for each one. Ermin initially worked as a university research administrator. He eventually established his business as a real estate broker.

As though on schedule, the Oro children paddled their own canoes while immersed in the pursuit of their academic degrees. They were ever mindful that, without finishing the goals of higher education, they would not be able to seal their future adequately.

Answers to the fabled American dream are not all tangible is what Lor and Ermin had thoroughly convinced themselves. That dream is not measured in possessing grand real estate properties. It is not evaluated by bank deposits. It is not measured by material comforts. It is not judged by the number of travels to points of interest throughout the globe.

The veritable quest was for that one yardstick that involved attaining the goals of higher education, one that locks in a person firmly for life, ensuring that future for himself or herself, his or her children, and his or her children's children and firming up those same hopes that ferried this person from another country to a new land.

On her own, Lor felt she had navigated oceans from those of the East Pacific to the West Pacific, truly to a new land where future problems would seek solutions not only for the older generations but for those yet to come.

With the boundless help of divine providence that directs the fate of mankind and nations, their three children along with them, Lor and Ermin continued to pursue what they could, thanks to their love for education and training spurred by personal discipline.

Their eldest, a son, is a Superior Court judge of Los Angeles County. His siblings, likewise graduate school finishers, both acquired their respective graduate degrees from top-tier institutions in a year's time instead of the usual two-year period as they pushed on with their will to complete graduate school.

When Lor first came to the United States of America, calling it the Promised Land, she felt it palpably. With the children, she prayed they would not veer away from the goals of education on which their future was set. They didn't. They achieved in their own modest manner.

As the decades have proven, the third generation has likewise come forward to respond to the call of education. The oldest member of their third generation, a granddaughter, received her bachelor's degree in legal studies and social work from the University of California, Berkeley (CAL). She went on for a juris doctorate degree from the City University of New York (CUNY) and is a member of the California State Bar. Her sibling, another granddaughter, received her bachelor's degree likewise from CAL and earned her master's degree and teaching credential in education from UC-Irvine. Their other sibling, a grandson, received his professional degree in microbiology from UC-Santa Barbara. Another grandson, an alumnus of the US Naval Academy in Annapolis, has served in Iraq and other assignments as a naval air training officer.

Following in their older cousins' footsteps, the youngest grandsons likewise have ascended the educational ladder. The older grandson, a graduate of Maine's Bowdoin College, is in the doctoral program at Columbia University. His younger sibling received his bachelor's degree from The New School, New York City.

Lor and Ermin were fully aware of their mission in life. As they pursued their respective professions, they drew from their own dreams and prayed for the realization of their children's aspirations as well. Were it not for the power of the written word, the world of Lor and Ermin would never have commenced. Never unfolded; not the manner by which each chapter in their own book of life would have been written and unwritten.

Inevitably, each time Valentine's Day would appear on the scene, they would refer to 1948 when written communication visibly made its very first appearance, not long after the conclusion of World War II.

From 1965, when their professional lives were ensconced, Lor and Ermin lodged their crucial hopes that, as worthy Americans, they would render their best, to do what they were capable of doing in their very modest manner. As each day wore on, they guided their three children to be grateful for America's gifts while they knew permanence was theirs in their adopted land.

Lor and Ermin never abandoned their fondest dreams about freedom and education. When Lor and Ermin reviewed what they mulled together as the legacy they had unwittingly set upon and strove for in the more than six decades together since they exchanged marriage vows on Hearts' Day 1952, the story could not be recounted without how theirs grew out and nurtured by writing, how the power of communication came through for them will be enshrined in the memory of their heirs.

Theirs is the story of hearts that dared, meant to live forever as the generations that continue to come after them will remember. It is how the journey undertaken by Lor and Ermin created through writing, morphed into life. It will be told and retold by the generations after them.

Writing for *Gavel to Gavel*, a Los Angeles Superior Court journal, Rafael, oldest heir of Lor and Ermin, said:

> Like many Americans or future Americans born with strange names in strange-sounding places, I and now my own family still have the same hopes and dreams my parents had. With thanks this time to those with the power to have made it possible and plain old luck, I am both proud and challenged to work in a free society committed to the rule of law and the ideal of justice.

CPSIA information can be obtained
at www.ICGtesting.com
Printed in the USA
LVHW03s1433091018
592979LV00001B/258/P